DIY FURNITURE 2

A step-by-step guide

CHRISTOPHER STUART

DIY FURNITURE 2

A step-by-step guide

CHRISTOPHER STUART

Laurence King Publishing

LAURENCE KING

Published in 2014 by
Laurence King Publishing Ltd
361–373 City Road
London EC1V 1LR

email: enquiries@laurenceking.com
www.laurenceking.com

A catalog record for this book is available
from the British Library.

ISBN: 978-1-78067-367-7

Design: Jason Ribeiro
Series design: Jon Allan
Senior editor: Peter Jones

Printed in China

1.
SHELVES AND STORAGE

You're into design, so you probably have lots of shiny objects glittering about that you've collected along the way. No worries, we've got you covered. Strap yourself in for the tension-held XX shelf design by Naoya Matsuo. Dust off grandma's antique dinnerware and show it off on Iolo, a Welsh dresser (or china hutch for those of you west of the Atlantic) that was designed and made using only a few tools. Spanish designer, Blanca Ortiz shows us how to bring the outdoors in with her flower cart—a romantic-looking shelf that is made using only one wood profile. Don't want your knick-knackery where the little ones can get to it? Tuck it all away behind the corrugated doors of Sine Cabinet. The translucent quality of the corrugated plastic shows off the beautiful skeletal-like construction of the cabinet, so it looks great empty or full.

XX SHELVES

NAOYA MATSUO

Naoya's XX Shelves are taken from his "Less Machine More Hand" collection, which focuses on DIY store materials and low-tech tools for production, or "forms from structures with general materials", as Naoya describes them. XX embodies the concept well. The shelves have simple components: just one sheet of plywood cut into three, four wooden rods, and two strips of polypropylene tape. The tape strips, which also act as a design accent, form braces to keep the structure stable.

Naoya exhibited XX as one of three pieces of knock-down furniture at the Stockholm Furniture Fair in 2011. Every time he exhibits in foreign countries, he designs knock-down pieces and carries them all by hand to save costs.

XX has been launched by a producer in Japan. The initial design was too difficult for a DIY project, so Naoya created an easier DIY version, which is the one shown here.

You will need:

Materials

_Four wooden dowels, 1⅛in diameter, at least 36in long

_Two lashing straps, 1in wide, 65in long

_One sheet of plywood, 1 x 36 x 36in

_Twelve ⅛in (M4) sharp-point truss-head nails, 2½in long

_Six ⅛in (M4) sharp-point truss-head nails, 1in long

_Eighteen ⅛in (M4) plastic caps for nails

Tools

_Scissors

_Hammer

_Saw

_Drill

_Drill bit, 1¼in diameter

1

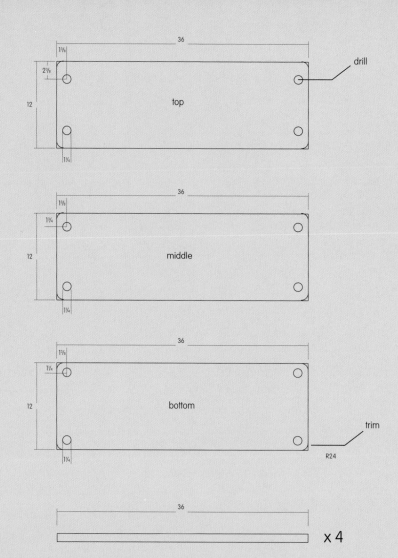

36

1⅜

2⅜

12

top

drill

36

1⅜

1¾

12

middle

1¼

36

1⅜

1¼

12

bottom

trim

1¼

R24

_Cut the 1in plywood to the following
sizes:
_Three x 36 x 12in
_Drill four 1¼in holes in each board
as shown (be careful to drill them
straight/vertical). The holes are
slightly bigger to allow the dowel to
insert at a slight angle). Notice that
the placement varies on each one:
Top, 2⅜in from edge
Middle, 1¾in from edge
Bottom, 1¼in from edge
_Cut the four dowels to 36in long
_Use a jigsaw or sander to trim the
corners of the boards as shown,
approximately 1in radius.

36

x 4

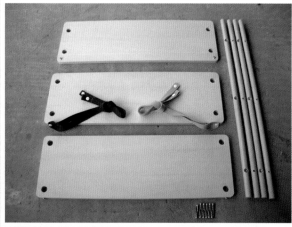

2

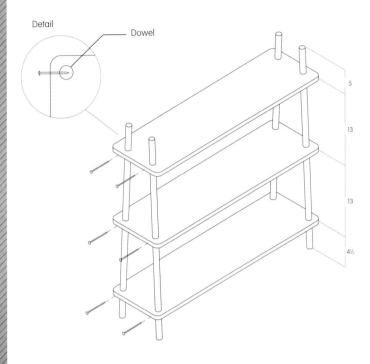

Detail

Dowel

5

13

13

4½

_Insert the four dowels through the holes and space as shown
(you can cut wooden spacers and place them between the
shelves to make assembly easier).
_Hammer the 2½in-long nails into the sides of the shelves so
they go into the dowel, as shown in the detail.

3

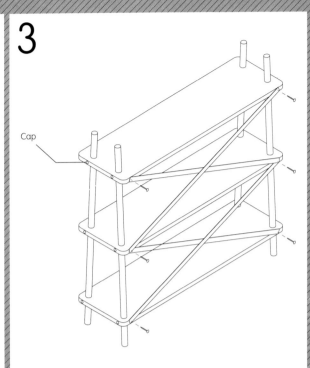

Cap

_Nail one end of a lashing strap to the back of the top shelf.
Pulling it tight, stretch it diagonally across and down to the next shelf,
and nail it in place with a 1in-long nail.
Stretch it once more across and down to the next shelf and nail
it in place.
_Repeat on the opposite side with the other lashing strap.
_Use scissors to cut the excess strap.
_Use a hammer to cap over the nails.

4

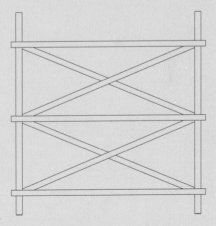

_Fill your XX with objects and enjoy!

SINE CABINET

DIK SCHEEPERS

The inspiration for the Sine Cabinet was twofold. Firstly, in the area of the Netherlands where Scheepers grew up, flowers are sold along the streets. You help yourself to a bunch and leave your money in a tin can. The flowers are often housed in shabby booths made from leftover corrugated PVC, which Scheepers always found disappointing, since this is potentially such an attractive material, especially when light shines through it.

Scheepers' second observation was that when people first buy a cabinet they tend to keep it well organized, and it looks pretty good standing in a room. But after a while, it tends to disappear into its surroundings as all sorts of things are stuffed into it. It becomes just another cabinet.

He wanted to make a cabinet that couldn't be put against a wall, but instead jumped off it, forcing its owner to keep noticing it. That's why the frame of the Sine Cabinet extends beyond just the rear of the cabinet. This cabinet will also change over time—the fuller it gets, the less the transparent PVC will reveal.

People think of corrugated PVC as a throwaway material. By combining it with a traditional material for quality furniture, however, that feeling changes. After a few experiments with other types of wood, Scheepers settled on oak—providing a combination that enables people to see just how nice corrugated PVC can be.

You will need:

Materials

_Oak (new or old furniture), a total of 197ft in 2 x 2in battens

_Corrugated PVC, cut into the following panels: 17⅛ x 56¼in (panel AA), 18 x 56¼in (BB), 13 x 56¼in (CC), 12¼ x 35in (DD)

_Wood glue

_Brass screws and hinges

_Four magnets

_Nails

Tools

_Saw

_Router

_Planer

_Jointer

_Sander

_Drill

_Grinder

_Breathing mask

1

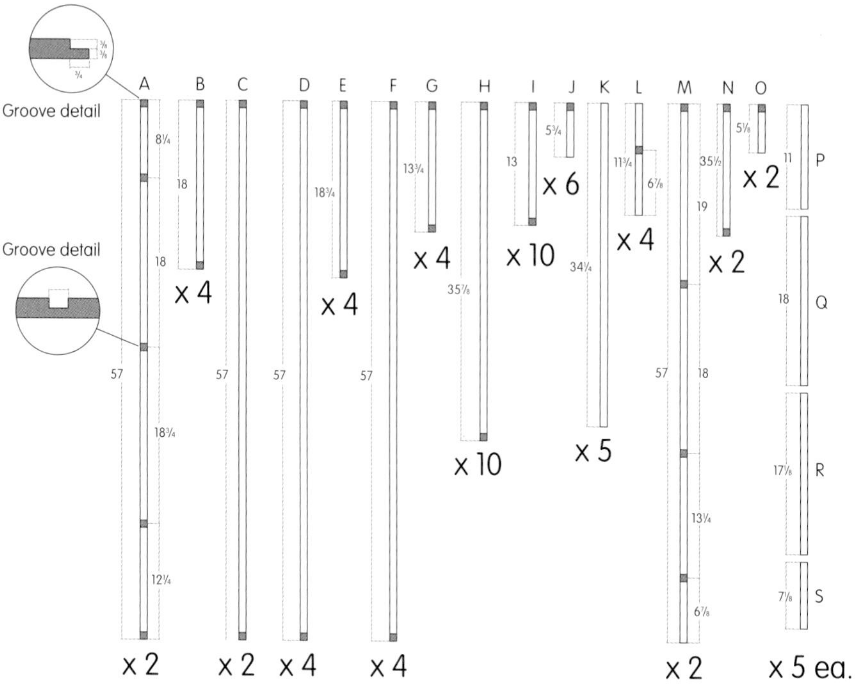
Groove detail
⅜
⅜
¾
A B C D E F G H I J K L M N O
Groove detail
8¼
18
18
18¼
12¼
57
18
57
57
18¾
57
13¾
35⅞
13
5¾
34¼
11¾
6⅞
57
18
19
13¼
6⅞
35½
5⅛
11
18
17⅛
7⅛
P
Q
R
S
x 4
x 4
x 4
x 10
x 6
x 4
x 2
x 2
x 10
x 5
x 2
x 2
x 4
x 4
x 2
x 5 ea.

Wooden battens

_Use the planer and jointer to make sure the cross section of the oak is consistently ¾ x ¾in.
_Cut the timber to the following lengths, making sure to add the half-lap groove details highlighted in gray:

Back panels (parts A–C)
_Two x 57in (part A)
_Four x 18in (part B)
_Two x 57in (part C)

Door panels (parts D & E)
_Four x 57in (part D)
_Four x 18¾in (part E)

Side panels (parts F & G)
_Four x 57in (part F)
_Four x 13¾in (part G)

Horizontal panels (parts H & I)
_Ten x 35⅞in (part H)
_Ten x 13in (part I)

Structure (parts J–S)
_Six x 5¾in (part J)
_Five x 34¼in (part K)
_Four x 11¾in (part L)
_Two x 57in (part M)
_Two x 14in (part N)
_Two x 5⅛in (part O)
_Five x 11in (part P)
_Five x 18in (part Q)
_Five x 17⅛in (part R)
_Five x 7⅛in (part S)

2

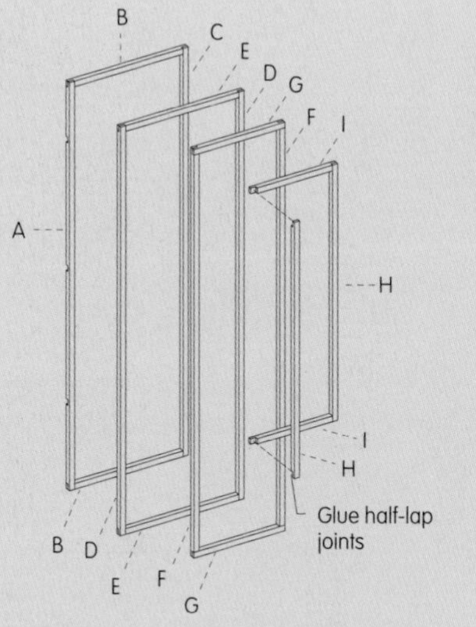
B
C
E
D
G
F
I
A
H
I
H
Glue half-lap joints
B D
E F
G

Assemble the panels as shown:

Back panels (parts A–C)
_Use glue at each of the half-lap joints on parts A–C to assemble one back panel (panel A). Clamp and let it dry completely.
_For the second back panel (panel AA*), flip parts A and C, then glue and clamp.

Door panels (parts D & E)
_Use glue at each of the half-lap joints on parts D and E to assemble one door panel (panel BB). Clamp and let it dry. Repeat for the second door panel (also panel BB).

Side panels (parts F & G)
_Use glue at each of the half-lap joints on parts F and G to assemble one side panel (panel CC). Clamp and let it dry. Repeat for the second side panel (also panel CC).

Horizontal panels (parts H & I)
_Use glue at each of the half-lap joints on parts H and I to assemble one horizontal panel (panel DD). Clamp and let it dry. Repeat four more times (panels DD*).

3

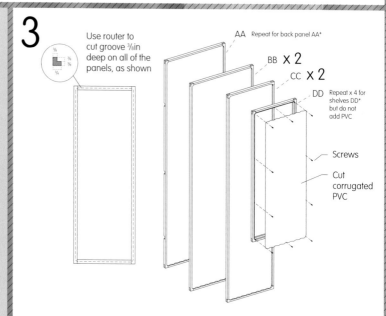

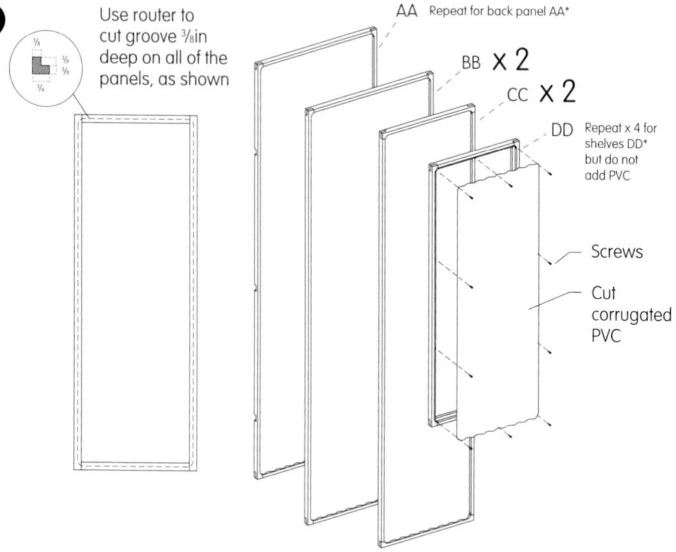
Use router to cut groove ⅜in deep on all of the panels, as shown
AA Repeat for back panel AA*
BB x 2
CC x 2
DD Repeat x 4 for shelves DD* but do not add PVC
Screws
Cut corrugated PVC

_Using the router, cut a ⅜in deep groove, ⅜in inset from the outside edge of each panel, as shown above, making sure to round the corners. Add the groove detail to all panels AA–DD, including panels AA* and DD*.
_Using the grinder, cut the corrugated PVC to size in the following quantities:
_Two x panels AA and AA* 17⅛ x 56¼in
_Two x panels BB 18 x 56¼in
_Two x panels CC 13 x 56¼in
_One x panel DD 12¼ x 35in. The four panels DD* with the groove detail will later have wood planks inserted in the grooves to be used as shelves. Note: do not use a saw because it will cause small pieces to break off. Also make sure you wear the correct breathing mask since dust and fumes may be produced.
_Clean the edges of the PVC panels prior to installing. Predrill small holes to prevent splitting and attach the panels with screws.

4

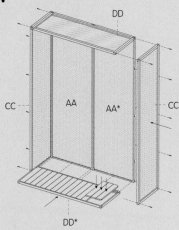

Assembling the cabinet

_Attach panels AA and AA* together with glue and screws. Make sure that the three half-lap grooves are on the outside edge of both panels.
_Attach both panels CC to the outside edges of AA and AA* with glue and screws.
_Attach the top panel DD with glue and screws.
_Cut thin boards of oak and attach the oak planks to the groove panel DD*. You will need to cut additional thin boards of oak for the four remaining panels DD*, since they will be used for shelves later.
_Attach the completed panel DD* with glue and screws at the base of the cabinet.

5

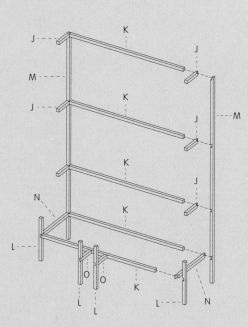

_Assemble the cabinet frame as shown, using glue and screws.

6

_Put the cabinet on a block of wood to support it while you slide the frame in place. Use glue and screws to attach the frame and cabinet. Make sure you line up the frame with the grooves on the back of the cabinet for greater rigidity.
_Add screws from inside the cabinet, attaching it to both the horizontal and vertical frame pieces.

7

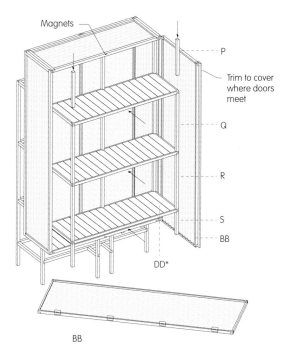

Trim to cover where doors meet

_Use oak parts P–S as corner columns for supporting each of the shelves (parts DD*) as shown above. There should be a total of five columns supporting each shelf: four columns in each corner and one column in the back center. Use glue and nails as necessary to attach the shelves and columns to the inside of the cabinet.
_Mount the doors (parts BB) using four hinges on each door, and adjust the hinges to create even spacing on all sides.
_Cut a thin piece of trim to length and attach it to one of the doors (parts BB) with a slight overlap to cover where the doors meet when closed.
_Drill small pockets where the inside corners of the doors meet the cabinet body, and insert four magnets to help keep the cabinet doors in place when shut.

8

_Store all of your favorite keepsakes in the cabinet and enjoy!

25X25

BLANCA ORTIZ

25X25 is a piece of wooden furniture—pine or beech—designed to honor a reading space and the activity of reading itself. The best place to read and relax is near a window. This also happens to be the best place to plant flowers, which in turn help to create a relaxed atmosphere. The 25x25 flower trolley combines both elements to create the perfect reading spot at home.

This project was designed to be easy for anyone to build, so all the components can be found in any hardware store, and can be replaced if necessary. Its assembly process is very simple too, and uses just screws.

The name 25X25 comes from the metric size of the strip section of the wood used to create the whole structure.

You will need:

Materials

_Wooden battens, 1 x 1in, 37¾ft total length

_Four lengths stainless steel L profile, 1 x 1 x 39½in, with hole openings of 30mm

_White felt, ⅛in thick, 4 x 8in

_48 wood screws, ¼in-diameter head, 1⅝in long

_Ten wood screws, ¼in-diameter head, ¾in long

_Metal cross brace, 3¼ft (1m) long (can be found at IKEA—Observatör)

_Glue for felt

_Two swivel wheels, 1⅛in diameter, 2in total height

Tools

_Drill bit for predrilling screws

_Saw

1

x 2 ——————————— 39½ ——————————— A

x 2 ——————————— 37½ ——————————— B

x 2 ——————————— 31½ ——————————— C | 2

x 4 ——————— 23½ ——————— D

x 14 ——— 10 ——— E

Subtract wheel height

Use a saw to cut the 1 x 1in wooden battens into the following lengths:
_Two x 39½in (part A)
_Two x 37½in (subtract your wheel height from 39½in) (part B)
_Two x 31½in (part C)
_Four x 23½in (part D)
_Fourteen x 10in (part E)

2

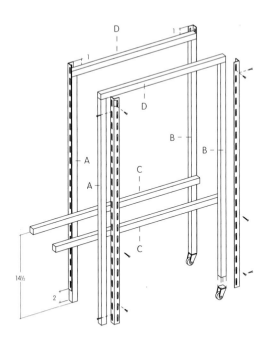

Assembling the sides
_Use one 39½in length of L-shaped steel profile to
connect one part A, D, and B, leaving a 1in space
above part D (you can use a scrap piece of 1in board
as a spacer).
_Repeat for the other side, but note that the steel is on the
opposite side.
_Attach your wheels.
_Place the cross pieces (parts C) 14½in from the bottom
and attach by screwing through the appropriate hole
in the metal, checking to make sure you attach to the
insides (opposite the steel).

3

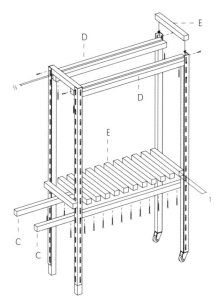

Connecting the two sides
_Place two of the 10in pieces (parts E) on top of your
 assembled sides, screwing together through the
 appropriate holes in the metal.
_Attach two more 23½in battens (parts D) to the bottom
 side of parts E by screwing from underneath into parts E
 and spacing ⅜in from the existing parts D.
_Attach the remaining twelve 10in battens (parts E) by
 screwing through the underside of parts C, spacing
 1in apart.

4

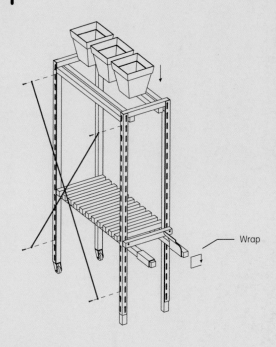

Wrap

_Use screws to attach the X-shaped metal support to the
 side you choose as the back.
_Cut the felt into two pieces, 4 x 4in.
_Use glue to attach and wrap it around parts C.
_Place your planters.

5

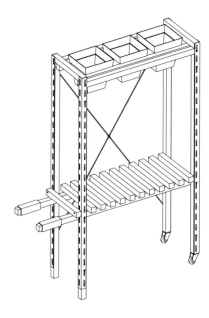

_Fill with plants, wheel to your favorite spot, and enjoy!

IOLO

THOMAS JENKINS

Iolo is a Welsh dresser that started out as a commission for the studio's local café. The café owners didn't have a massive budget so Jenkins' studio set about creating a solution that could be manufactured internally in their prototype workshop, which has only a few pieces of machinery.

This meant creating a very simple system using only the tools the designers had available to them, as well as keeping manufacturing time as short as possible. The studio was able to create this dresser with just a router, a miter saw, and a pillar drill.

You will need:

Materials

_Plywood, ⅞in thick

_Small-head finish nails, 2in long

_Copper pipe, ½in diameter

_Wooden dowels, 1¾in diameter

_Wood glue

_Drawer slides no larger than 13¼in

_Rubber or plastic feet that nail on —1⅝in

Tools

_Saw

_Drill

_Drill bit, ½in diameter

_Drill bit, 1¾in diameter

_Drill bit, ¼in diameter

_Router

_Round ½in router bit

_Round ⅜in router bit

_Hammer

1

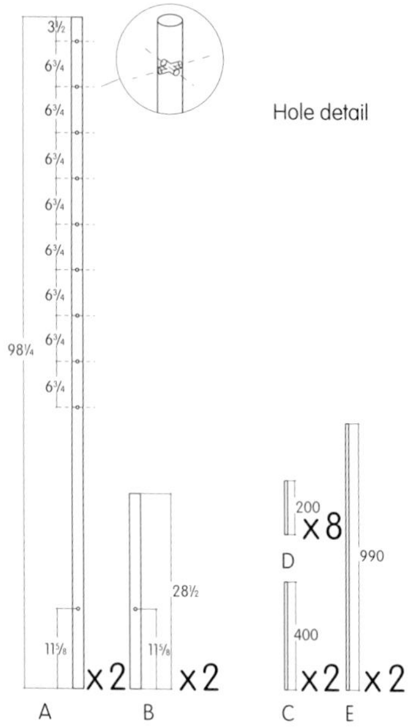

Dowels

Copper pipe

Dowels and copper pipe

Cut the 1¾in dowels to the following lengths:
_Two x 98¼in (part A)
_Two x 28½in (part B)
_Use a ½in drill bit to make holes as shown.
All the holes that are shown facing are drilled on the front side. Where horizontal dotted lines are shown (upper portion of part A), ½in holes need to be drilled from the side (perpendicular to the holes from the front side), see detail. Cut the ½in copper pipe to the following lengths:
_Two x 15¾in (part C)
_Eight x 7⅞in (part D)
_Two x 39in (part E)

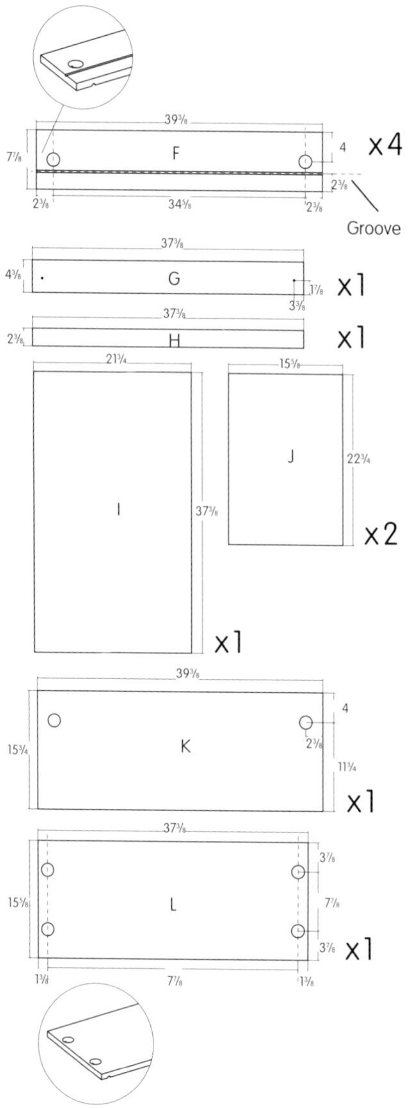

Shelves and cabinet

Cut the ⅞in plywood to the following sizes:
_Four x 39⅜ x 7⅞in (part F)
_One x 37⅜ x 4⅜in (part G)
_One x 37⅜ x 2⅜in (part H)
_One x 37⅜ x 21¾in (part I)
_Two x 22¾ x 15⅝in (part J)
_One x 39⅜ x 15¾in (part K)
_One x 37⅜ x 15⅝in (part L)
_Use a router with a ½in round bit to cut two half-circle-shaped grooves that run the shorter distance on the bottom side of parts F and L. Parts F will get these 2⅜in from each end as shown. The copper tubes will rest in these grooves.
Part L will get these 1⅜in from each end, as shown.
_Use an ⅜in round bit to cut a groove the length of the board, 2⅜in from the front edge, as shown.
_Use a drill and a 1¾in bit to cut holes through parts F, K, and L, as shown.
_Use a ¼in drill bit to cut two holes in board G, as shown.

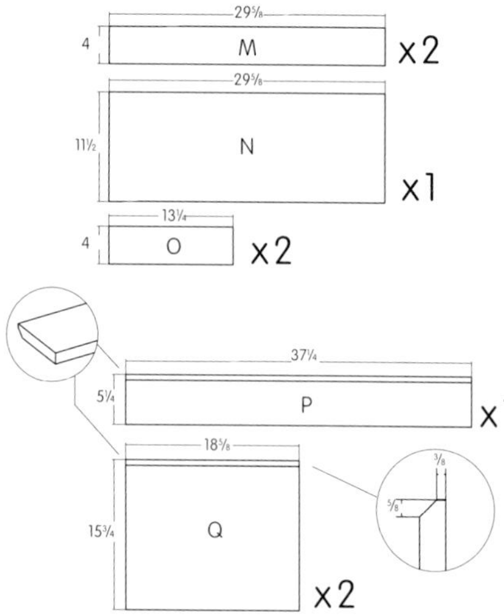

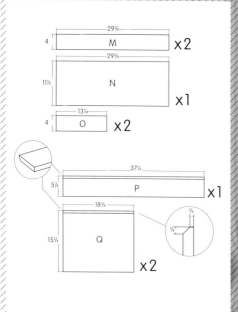

Doors and drawer

Cut the ⅞in plywood to the following sizes:
_Two x 29⅝ x 4in (part M)
_One x 29⅝ x 11½in (part N)
_Two x 13¼ x 4in (part O)
_One x 37¼ x 5¼in (part P)
_Two x 18⅝ x 15¾in (part Q)
Use a saw or router to bevel one edge of parts P and Q, as shown above. These will be the top edges of the doors (Q x 2) and the bottom of the drawer face (P).

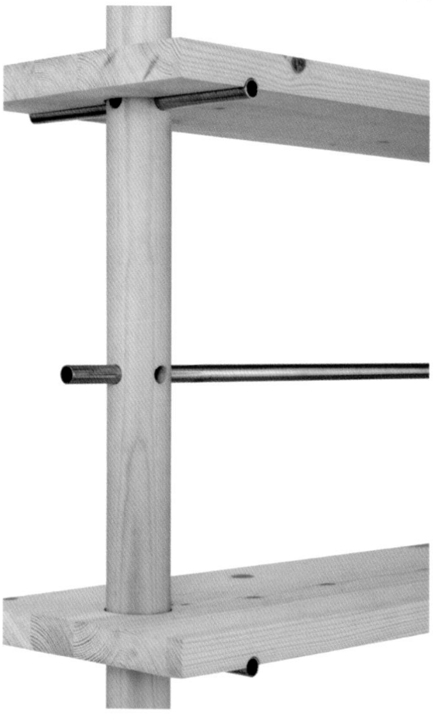

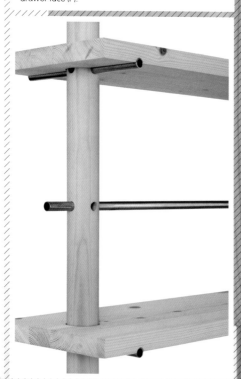

2

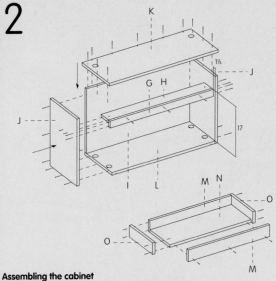

Assembling the cabinet

This is easier if the cabinet is laid on its back (part I).
_Attach the bottom (part L) with grooves out, using glue at the seams and nailing together with finish nails.
_Attach the sides (parts J) and the top (part K).
_Attach the divider and leg support (parts G and H) as shown. First, attach part H to part G, making flush along the top edge and nail in place. Then, spacing 1⅛in from the front edge of the cabinet and measuring up 17in from the top of part L to the top edge of part H, nail in place through parts J.

Assembling the drawer box

This will be easier with the bottom (part N) laying flat.
_Attach the sides (parts O) and the front and back (parts M) using glue at the seams and nailing together with finish nails.

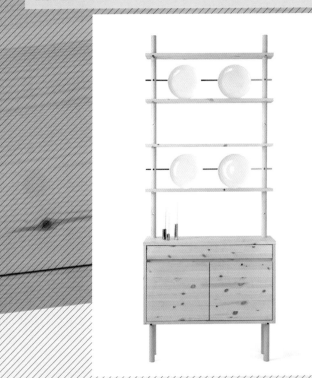

3

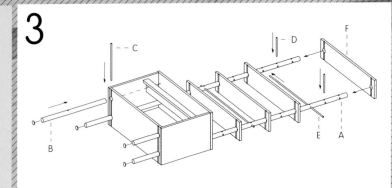

Assembling the legs and shelving

_Insert the rear legs (parts A) through the bottom of the cabinet until the last hole is just visible.
_Insert the front legs (parts B) the same way. The front legs should hit the divider frame just as the last hole becomes visible.
_Insert two copper pipes (parts C) into the bottom holes of the legs, going through the front legs (parts B), then through the rear legs (parts A).
_Slide each shelf (parts F) over the rear legs, with the side with two grooves facing down. Pin each shelf in place with the shorter copper pipes (parts D), by inserting into the holes in parts A, beneath each shelf.
_Add the longer copper pipes (parts E) by inserting in the holes above each shelf that you wish to hold plates.
_Optionally add feet.

4

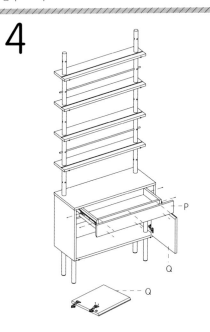

_Stand the cabinet upright and attach the drawer, using top-mounting drawer slides. The drawer box should be ¾in from the underside of the top of the cabinet (part K).
_Align the drawer face (part P) to the drawer box with the bevel side down and facing in. Space it evenly on the top and sides, then attach using glue and nails.
_Mount the doors (parts Q) with the bevel side up and facing in. Use inset-style door hinges and follow the hinge directions for their placement. Adjust the hinges to create even spacing on all sides.

5

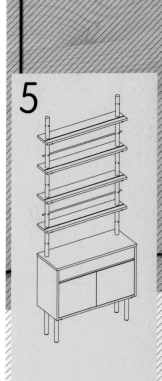

_Display your finest dinnerware and enjoy!

2.
TABLES AND DESKS

The hardware store isn't the only place to find readymade materials ripe for appropriation. Travis Ekmark found that the holes in the common pizza tray could act as predrilled locators to attach shelf brackets repurposed into table legs. The slender profile of Buchshop also utilizes existing shelving parts, but displays books instead of take-out pizza. Add a couple of wooden planks and it transforms into a work surface. Dominik Hehl offers a clever take on the trestle table, cutting each leg from one plank of wood and joining them with a piano hinge so that the wood appears to fold. Stacking wood is another build method used, as demonstrated in Telefonplan, which brings back childhood memories of creating log cabins with Tinkertoys. Niccolò Spirito shows us that PVC doesn't have to be relegated to the basement. Take it to the next level and build the PVC Table to accompany his other PVC contribution, the Diablo Chair.

ROHLINGTISCH

DOMINIK HEHL

In his latest works, Hehl acts in the spirit of a DIY maker, looking for *Rohlinge*—which translates as "raw materials"—that he can easily transform into useful objects. In German the word also means "rough guy", so it also has connotations of something rough and raw.

Hehl's aim was to design common, functional objects using raw materials with very few processes. This approach looks for simplicity within the production process and celebrates the chosen source material, whether it comes straight from nature or is industrially processed to some extent.

After spotting a yellow framework panel on a visit to a hardware store, Hehl was inspired to create a table. Rohlingtisch consists of collaged panels, with a metal profile only partially visible. Each table leg is cut from just one framework panel, although the assembly of the diagonally divided panels gives the impression of folded wood. Joined by a hinge, the two legs work like a trestle. The weight of the tabletop in turn stabilizes the position of the legs, so no fixing is necessary.

Any wood can be used to create your own Rohlingtisch!

You will need:

Materials

_Wood screws, ⅛ x 1¾in

_Wood glue

_Three framework panels, 60 x 20in

_Three framework panels, 80 x 20in

_Wood lacquer

_Two hinges, 2⅜– 3⅛ in wide (If you want to connect the legs to table, you will need four more)

Tools

_Saw

_Drill

1

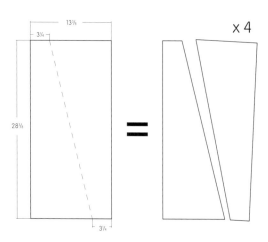

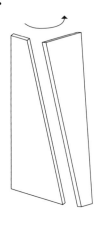

Legs
_Cut four pieces measuring 13⅜ x 28⅜in out of two 60 x
   20in framework panels.
_Cut each piece diagonally to make eight matching parts.

2

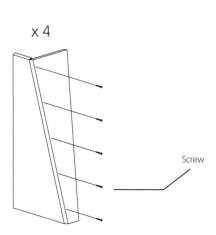

Screw

_Rotate one section as if you were folding it.
_Join the two divided parts orthogonally as shown,
   using wood glue on the joints and securing with screws.
_Repeat this so you have four identical legs in total.

3

_Lean two of the legs against each other and connect
   them with a hinge and screws. Repeat with the other
   two legs.

4

x 2

100

28

B

A

C

=

Doubled up

Tabletop

_To create the first layer, use one 20 x 80in panel (Part A). Cut the second 20 x 80in panel into two 8 x 80in pieces (Part B). Use one here and one on the second layer. Cut the remaining 20 x 60in panel into two 28 x 20in pieces (Part C), using one on the first layer and one on the second.

_You can use any type of tabletop. The example shown on page 27 used a framework panel, creating two patterned layers, which were doubled up by screwing them together from the bottom to make one thick top.

_The layout can be as shown.

5

_Seal the wood with lacquer (optional).
_Set the tabletop on the legs (attach using hinges if you wish), pull up some chairs and enjoy!

TELEFONPLAN

DANIEL FRANZÉN OF BUNKER HILL

Franzén's pieces almost always tells a story, which is very common in the design world today, but it was a different story when he first set up his office. When he presented his first piece of jewelry in 2005—a symbol joining the three Abrahamic religions (Judaism, Christianity, and Islam)—it was his way of telling the story of the world around us, but it was not appreciated by everyone at the time.

Telefonplan is both a celebration of the beauty of pine as it comes, straight from a lumberyard, and also a homage to Enzo Mari, the Italian furniture designer who often applies a DIY philosophy to his work. The idea was to create an inexpensive table that could be built by almost anyone.

The table, which was also constructed to incorporate a lamp, was included in the 2008 "Future Living" exhibition in Sweden.

You will need:

Materials

_Sixteen wooden (pine or other) dowels, 1¾in diameter, at least 31½in long

_Toughened glass top, ⅕–⅜in thick, 3½in radius, 35½ x 35½in with rounded corners

_Thirty-two screws, 2–2⅜in long

_Four small rubber feet for glass

_Wood glue

_Wooden plugs that fit the screw hole size (you can also make these yourself using a plug cutter and the scrap from the dowels)

Tools

_Drill

_Countersink bit

1

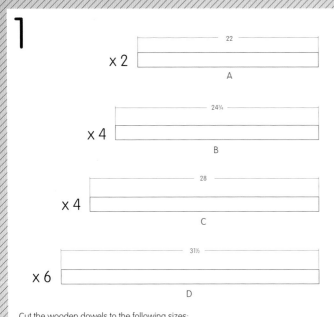

_Cut the wooden dowels to the following sizes:
_Two x 22in (part A)
_Four x 24¾in (part B)
_Four x 28in (part C)
_Six x 31½in (part D)

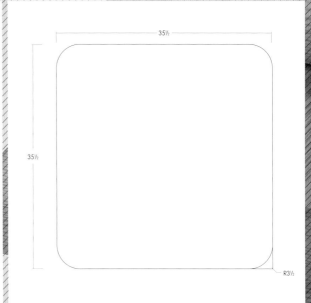

_Have your local glazier cut the glass to the above size and harden. The radius of the corner is 3½in.

2

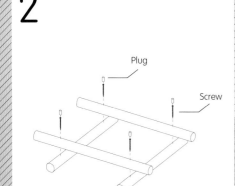

Plug

Screw

_Build the table upside down by stacking two parts A and two parts B to create the first section (refer to Fig. 1 for placement).
_Hold or clamp the parts firmly and drill through the top dowel and halfway down into the bottom one.
_If you want to hide the screws, use a countersink bit to drill a pocket (about ³⁄₈in deep) and plug the holes using a little wood glue.

Fig. 1

View 1

View 2

3

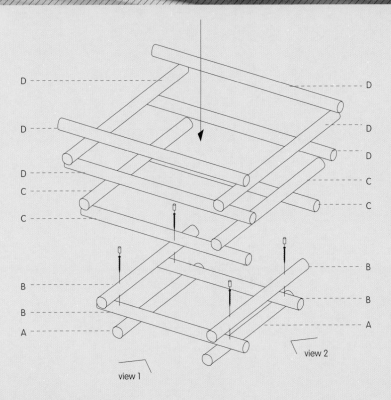

D

D

D

D

D

C

C

C

C

B

B

B

B

A

A

view 1

view 2

_Take the remaining two part B dowels and stack
them on top of the first section.
_Place two part C dowels on top of those and repeat this
pattern, screwing the dowels together as shown.

4

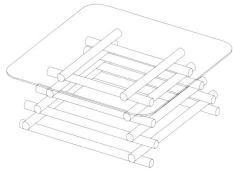

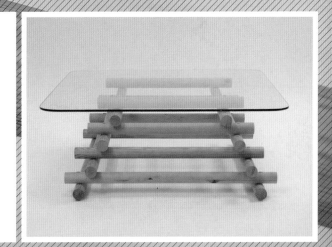

_Turn the frame over, add the glass top, and enjoy!
_Add the small rubber feet between the frame and the
glass if you want to keep the glass from sliding.

PIZZA TABLE

TRAVIS EKMARK

Should everything be designed from scratch? What happens when we edit the purpose of things we already have?

Atlanta-based Travis Ekmark has done just that, by transforming some simple, readymade pizza crispers into a nest of occasional tables. The tables are then finished with dark gray car primer and brass hardware.

You will need:

Materials

_One Chicago Metallic Commercial II traditional uncoated 14-inch pizza crisper

_Four shelving brackets, 12 x 14in

_Four 12/24 brass wing nuts

_Four 12/24 x ¼in slotted round top brass bolts, ¾in long

_Two 12-oz. spray cans of Rust-Oleum Matte Dark Gray automobile primer

Tools

_Drill press (or handheld drill, in a pinch)

_¼in drill bit

_High-grit sandpaper

_Cheap steel wire

_Wire cutters

_Old beach or bath towel

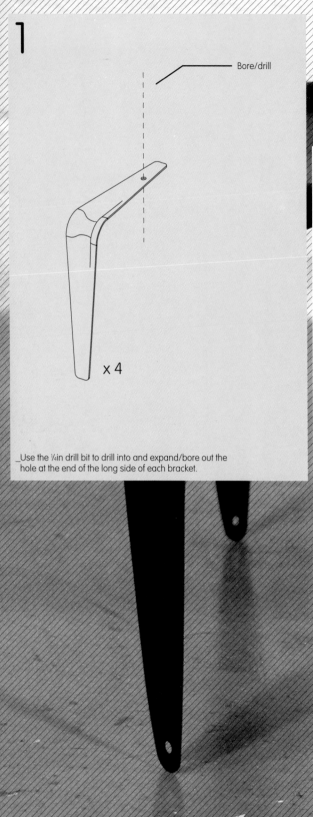

1

Bore/drill

x 4

_Use the ¼in drill bit to drill into and expand/bore out the hole at the end of the long side of each bracket.

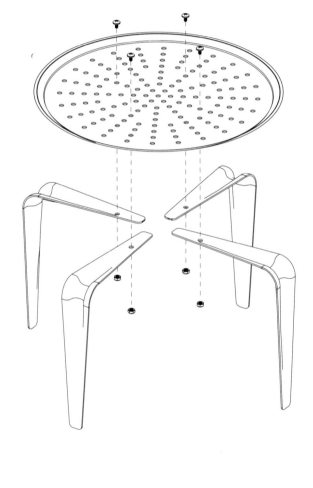

2

_Lightly sand the crisper and brackets to prepare for painting.
_Using steel wire and wire cutters, suspend the crisper and brackets in a paint booth or from a tree limb.
_Apply three to four even coats of car primer, leaving 30–60 minutes of drying time in between painting sessions.
_Lay a soft towel over the work surface and place the freshly dried parts on top. With the crisper upside down, begin attaching the brackets to the crisper, using the brass hardware.

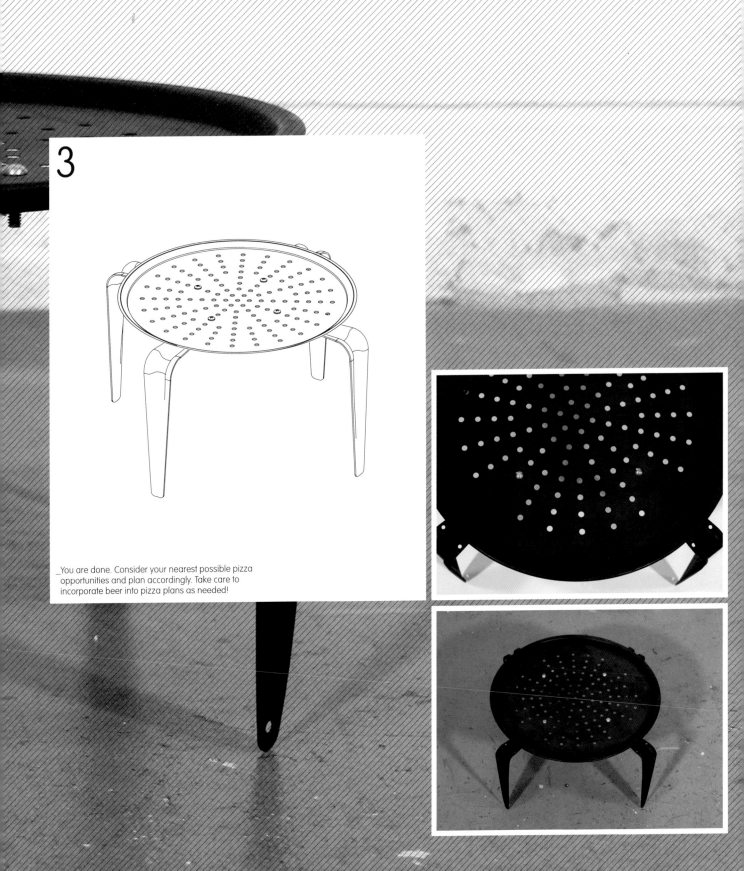

3

_You are done. Consider your nearest possible pizza opportunities and plan accordingly. Take care to incorporate beer into pizza plans as needed!

PVC TABLE

NICCOLÒ SPIRITO

In his laboratory in Milan, the young Italian designer Niccolò Spirito redefines the concept of recycling by using tools and waste materials to fashion new items.

He attempts to free materials from their usual functions in order to create new aesthetic results and emotional responses. Components such as PVC pipes, wrenches, and carpenter's clamps become the protagonists of new designs—sofas, tables, chairs, and lamps, all designed to stimulate the imagination and define new spaces.

The table shown here forms a companion piece to the PVC Diablo Chair on pp.50–53.

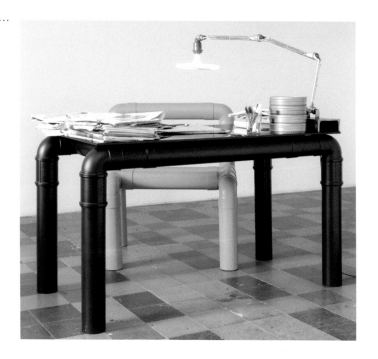

You will need:

Materials

_Seven PVC tubes, 4in diameter

_Four 4in 90-degree elbows (female on one end, male on the other) (part A)

_Four 4in Ts (male on one end, female on opposite end, female on perpendicular end) (part B)

_Four 4in sleeves (part C)

_Four suction cups

_One piece of black Plexiglas 60 x 28 x ⅜in

Tools

_PVC cleaner

_PVC glue

_Packing tape

_Can of expanding foam insulation

_Handsaw

_Saw for cutting tube like miter saw or handsaw with miter box (so you can cut straight)

_Drill with bit to match stem part of suction cup

1

_Cut the PVC to the following lengths:
_Two x 18in (part D)
_Two x 41in (part E)
_Four x 28in (part F)

2

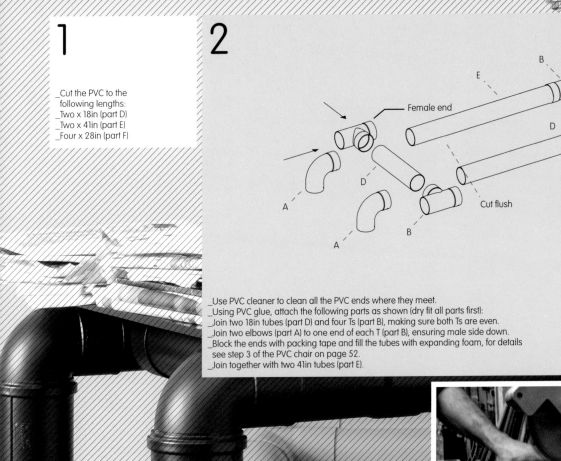

Female end

E

B

A

A

D

A

Male end

D

A

B

Cut flush

A

B

_Use PVC cleaner to clean all the PVC ends where they meet.
_Using PVC glue, attach the following parts as shown (dry fit all parts first):
_Join two 18in tubes (part D) and four Ts (part B), making sure both Ts are even.
_Join two elbows (part A) to one end of each T (part B), ensuring male side down.
_Block the ends with packing tape and fill the tubes with expanding foam, for details
 see step 3 of the PVC chair on page 52.
_Join together with two 41in tubes (part E).

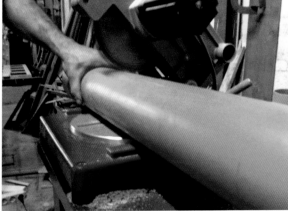

3

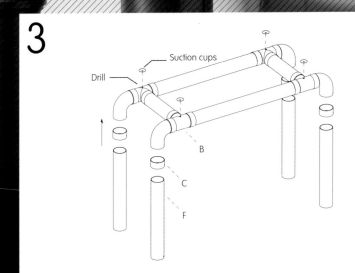

Suction cups

Drill

B

C

F

_Use PVC cleaner and glue and assemble the legs as shown:
_Join four sleeves (part C) and four 28in tubes (part F) to the male ends of
 the elbows (part A), ensuring the legs are vertical and even.
_Drill a hole in the top of each T (part B) to hold the suction cups (use a
 slightly smaller drill bit than the stem of the suction cup, so it is a tight fit).
_Fill the legs with expanding foam and cut excess flush with a handsaw.

4

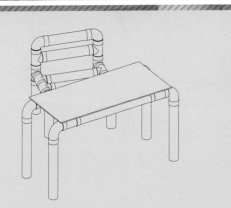

_Paint the table your favorite color, and add the Plexiglas top.
_Pull up a chair and get to work!

BUCHSHOP

STEPHANIE HORNIG, TINE HUHN, BODO PAHLKE, PASCAL HIEN

This modular system was originally created to provide a temporary exhibition space for over 500 books within 970 square feet. The Buchshop converts the standard shelving system—traditionally used in a vertical position—into a series of horizontal tables to become a presentation space, which allows visitors to open books directly and browse through them. The linear lines of tables, accessible from both sides, also provoke communication among visitors.

The tabletops consist of two hinged surfaces, and the use of standard components provides a very simple, cost-effective way of building a temporary structure.

You will need:

Materials

_Ten 9½in (240mm) Antonius brackets (IKEA)

_Four wall uprights, 35½in long

_Two spruce boards, 47 x 12 x ¾in

_Sixteen screws, ½in long

_Wood glue

_Tape

Tools

_Drill

_Metal snips

1

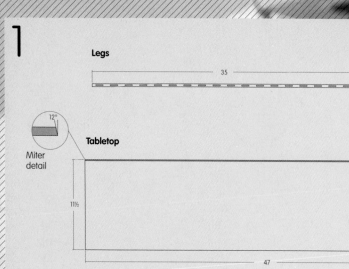

Legs

35   × 4

Tabletop

12°

Miter
detail

11½

47   × 2

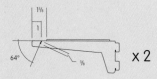

Shelf brackets

1⅛

1

64°   ⅜   × 2

Legs
_Cut the four wall uprights down to a length of 35in.
Tabletop
_Cut the two spruce boards down to a width of 11½in, at an angle of 12
degrees on one length of the board, as shown.
Shelf brackets
_Take two of the shelf brackets and make a ⅟₁₆in-wide cut at ⅜in long and at
an angle of 64 degrees, as shown.

2

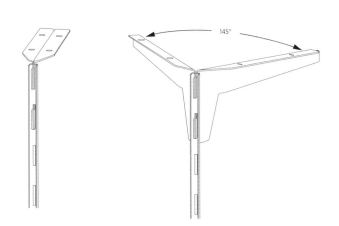

145°

_Press one left and one right bracket together into one
hole. Bend them away from each other to create an
angle of 145 degrees.

3

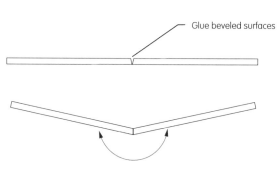

Glue beveled surfaces

_Align the prepared spruce boards with their beveled
edges together.
_Apply glue on the two beveled surfaces and fix both
pieces together. Use tape to help hold them together
while the wood glue dries.

4

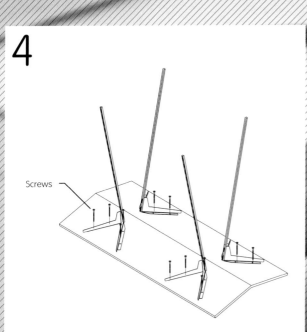

Screws

_Use screws to attach the legs to the tabletop.

5

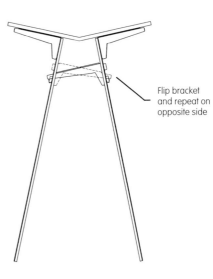

Flip bracket and repeat on opposite side

_Put one of the cut brackets a few holes down from the top.
_Flip the second cut bracket, and put it a few holes down from the top on the opposite side.

6

_Flip the table over and use it to hold all of your favorite magazines!

7

_You can also cut additional spruce boards to the correct width and place them on the angled surfaces to create a flat work surface.
_Place your laptop on the flat tabletop and enjoy!

3. SEATING

This chapter could easily be renamed "process and materials". With five different approaches to creating seating, and supply lists that may have you scratching your head, you'll want to try your hand at each one. If you are new to this making thing and don't know where to start, try the Diablo Chair. You don't need plumbing experience to make this PVC seat. Ever wondered what you should do with that half-used bag of concrete you've been storing in the garage? The aptly named Leftovers stools put it to good use, along with other job remnants you might have lying around. Studio Swine shows us how to manufacture a Sea Chair by remelting and pressing plastic that has washed ashore, while a straightforward design proudly featuring OSB as the primary material deserves an equally straightforward name like Chair. If you need to warm up to low-brow materials, then this quilted blanket chair cover is one to try. Or if swinging is more your style and you've always wanted to learn macramé, Ladies & Gentlemen Studio's Ovis Macramé Hanging Chair should tie you over.

OVIS MACRAMÉ HANGING CHAIR

LADIES & GENTLEMEN STUDIO

Chairs must perform two fundamental functions—support and comfort—and these functions are addressed in varying ratios by different designers.

The Ovis Macramé Hanging Chair's frame and sling construction provides a fresh way of addressing these opposing functions. Hard machined materials (metal and wood) are paired with soft textural ones (cotton ropes) to create a rigid structural frame that is intersected by a flowing woven sling. The result is a balance that feels at once supportive and comfortable.

You will need:

Materials

_Sixteen ¼in cotton twist cords, 28ft long

_One ½in cotton twist cord, 17ft long

_One ½in cotton twist cord, 20ft long

_Two 2in-diameter hardwood dowels, 29in long

_One 1½in-diameter hardwood dowel, 24in long

_1in-diameter copper tubing with ¹⁄₁₆in walls, 90in long

_Four brass wood screws, #8 x 1¾in

_Two screw hooks & rope to secure chair frame against the wall while creating the sling (optional)

_One stainless screw hook with at least ³⁄₈in diameter and 2¾in length of threaded surface (for attachment to ceiling)

_One brass marine snap hook, 3½in or more

_ ½in rope to hang from ceiling hook (length depends on height)

_Brass tube 32mm diameter, 76mm long

Tools

_Saw

_Metal saw for copper tubing

_Drill or drill press

_1in, ¾in, ³⁄₈in, ¹⁄₈in drill bits

_Scissors

_Masking tape

1

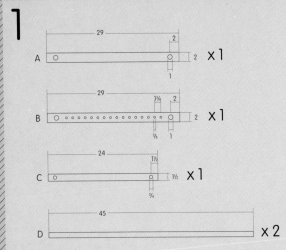

A — 29 — 2 — 2 x 1 — 1

B — 29 — 1¾ — 2 — 2 x 1 — ³/₈ — 1

C — 24 — 1½ — 1½ x 1 — ¾

D — 45 — x 2

Cut the wooden dowels to the following sizes:
_Two x 29in (parts A and B)
_One x 24in (part C)
Cut the copper tubes to the following size:
_Two x 45in (part D)
_Drill holes in the A, B, and C dowels as shown, making
  sure the holes are perfectly in line and parallel.

2

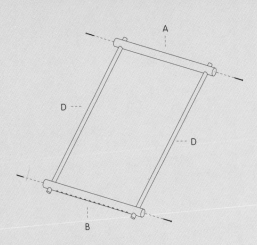

_Slide the copper tubes (parts D) into the 1in holes on each side of the 2in
  dowels (parts A and B).
_At the center of where the 2in dowels (parts A and B) and copper tubes (parts
  D) intersect, secure the frame with the brass screws (predrill the holes using a
  ⅛in bit prior to screwing in).
_Temporarily hang the top of the chair frame against a wall to keep the chair
  stable during the macramé process (see Fig. 1). Part A should be at the top.

3

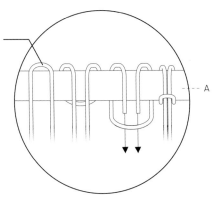

¼in cord

A

_Fold one of the ¼in twist cords in the center
  and wrap it around the top of part A to make
  a starting knot. Finish up with an overhand
  knot (see Fig. 2). Repeat this 16 times across
  the top.
_Make bundles with each separate rope length
  using tape so that they are easier to manage
  when macraméing, and to prevent the rope
  from fraying.

4

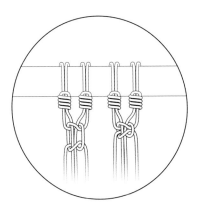

_A) Begin the first row by making alternating square
  knots. Take the first and fourth strands and make
  a square knot around the second and
  third strands (see Fig. 3). Then take the fifth and
  eighth strands, wrap them around the sixth
  and seventh strands, and continue this pattern
  until the end of row.
_B) Skip the first two strands and start a square knot
  at the third strand instead. Tie the knot at about 2in
  below the first row. Repeat making square knots
  across the row.
_Repeat Steps A & B, alternating the rows. Continue
  until the sling reaches 45in long.

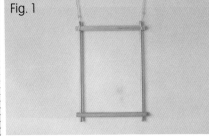

Fig. 1

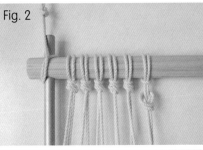

Fig. 2

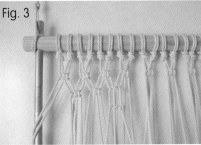

Fig. 3

5

_Once the sling reaches the ideal length of 45in, take the first two ropes and tie them together with an overhand knot. Repeat this with every two ropes until all are tied.
_Take each two-rope bundle and thread the ends through the ⅜in holes on the bottom dowel (part B). Tie another knot as close and tight to the dowel as possible and repeat for each two-rope bundle.
_Cut each rope to your preferred tassel length, and untwist the rope to make loose tassels. You can wet and press the rope with an iron to straighten out any kinks.

6

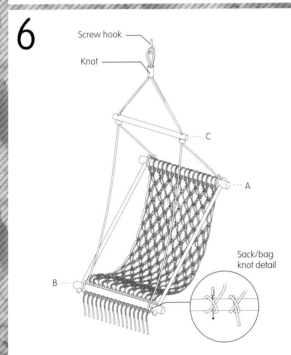

Screw hook

Knot

C

A

B

Sack/bag knot detail

_Take the 17ft and 20ft lengths of ½in-wide rope and find the center of each by folding them in half and taping the two sides together. Measure 6in down from the center fold and knot both rope sides together to make a loop for the top of the chair to hang from.
_Secure the threaded hook into a ceiling beam (make sure the beam can hold the load), then hang the desired length of rope.
_Slide the brass tube over the knot, then connect the rope to the top loop of the chair with the brass marine snap hook.
_For each side of the chair pair one 17ft and one 20ft section at each end of the knot and thread them together through the hole on each side of part C. Keep the rope straight and not twisted. Measure from the bottom of the upper knot and mark 18in down on all four ropes. On each side, take the two ropes and tie a knot at that 18in mark and below part C. The dowel will rest on these knots. Note: before fully tightening the knots, re-measure the ropes and check that both sides are even and that the dowel is level.
_Take the short ropes and make a sack or bag knot around part A on each side of the sling, inside the copper tubing. Ensure that the crisscross part of the knot faces the bottom side of the frame. Repeat the process with the long ropes around part B.

7

_Below the sack knots and the frame, use the remaining rope length to tie an overhand knot close and tight to the dowel to keep it secure. Cut the extra rope to your ideal length and untwist it to make tassels. You can wet and press the rope with an iron to straighten out any kinks.
_Take a seat, relax, and enjoy!

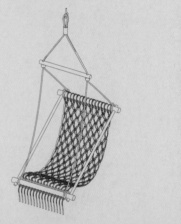

DIABLO CHAIR

NICCOLÒ SPIRITO

This chair was the first object that Niccolò made with PVC tubes. "I've always seen these PVC tubes and their connectors as objects capable of more versatile solutions; using them solely for drainage seemed a waste of their potential."

He bought some lengths of the PVC and some fittings, and after playing with the material, he realized that they lent themselves to various constructions. "They looked better than Lego."

The decision to build objects was immediate. The chair and table (see pp. 38–39) were born, and with them the idea of bringing a material back to life again.

The color of PVC drainpipe varies depending on whether it's used indoors or outdoors, as well as what country it is made in. You can choose to keep it in its molded color, or simply spray with a unique color.

You will need:

Materials

_Four PVC tubes, 4in diameter

_Four 4in 90-degree elbows (female on one end, male on the other) (part A)

_Eight 4in Ts (male on one end, female on opposite end, female on perpendicular end) (part B)

_Two 4in sleeves (part C)

Tools

_PVC cleaner

_PVC glue

_Packing tape

_Can of expanding foam insulation

_Handsaw

_Saw for cutting tube like miter saw or handsaw with miter box (so you can cut straight)

1

_Cut the PVC to the
following lengths:
_Three x 23½in (part D)
_One x 20in (part E)
_Four x 15¾in (part F)

2

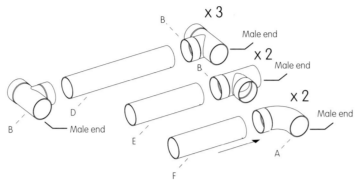

x 3

B

Male end

x 2

B

Male end

x 2

Male end

D

A

Male end

B

E

F

_Use PVC cleaner to clean all the PVC ends where they meet.
_Using PVC glue, attach the following parts as shown (dry fit
  all parts first):
_Join three 23½in tubes (part D) and six Ts (part B), making
  sure both Ts are even.
_Join two 15¾in tubes (part F) and two elbows (part A).
_Join two 20in tubes (part E) and two Ts (part B).

3

x 3

Female end

Scrap piece with
taped end

x 2

Female end

Female
end

Cut flush

x 2

_Use packing tape to tape one end of a scrap piece of PVC.
_Make two of these and use them to plug the female ends of the tube
  (this is to keep the expanding foam from filling these areas).
_Fill the tubes with expanding foam, cutting the excess off flush
  with a handsaw.
_Remove the scrap pieces.

4

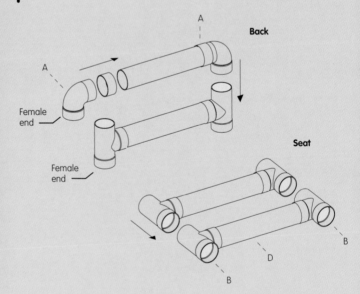

A

Back

A

Female
end

Female
end

Seat

D

B

B

B

_Use PVC cleaner to clean all the PVC ends where they meet.
_Using PVC glue, assemble the seat and back as shown.
_Join two previously assembled double-T units to make the seat.
_Join the two remaining elbows (part A), two sleeves (part C),
  and the remaining previously assembled double-T unit, as shown.

5

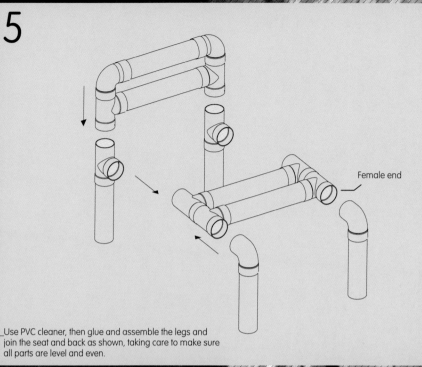

Female end

_Use PVC cleaner, then glue and assemble the legs and join the seat and back as shown, taking care to make sure all parts are level and even.

6

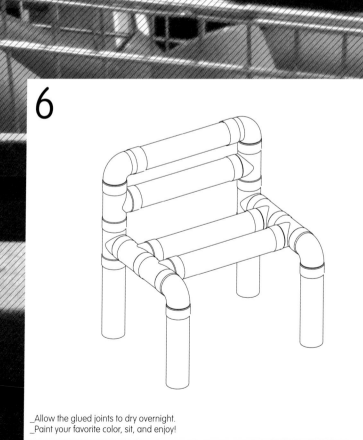

_Allow the glued joints to dry overnight.
_Paint your favorite color, sit, and enjoy!

SEA CHAIR

STUDIO SWINE

Ship stools were first made from wood or walrus tusks by seamen to occupy their time on long voyages; the Sea Chair uses plastic waste found at sea and a simple furnace to make a contemporary version. This open-source design uses readily available materials and basic DIY skills.

The United Nations estimates that some 100 million tons of plastic waste are floating in the world's oceans, a proportion of which washes up on coastlines around the globe. In 2012, Japan, for example, had more than 200,000 tons of plastic debris wash up along its shores. This abundance of plastic presents an opportunity—the material is delivered by the sea to coasts, where it can be collected and processed to make new products, thereby helping to clear the marine environment of plastic waste for good.

PRECAUTIONS
Since plastics emit toxic fumes when melted, some precautions are necessary. The lid and filter will help minimize exposure to fumes, but make sure you do any melting in a well-ventilated place, away from others—outside, if possible. Use a good mask and goggles to protect your eyes from the smoke. Hot plastic will stick to the skin, too, so always wear long sleeves and thick gloves (leather gardening gloves are fine).

You probably won't be able to easily identify a lot of the plastic you collect. The key is to collect a sizeable quantity of the same type so that it will mix well when melted. It's common to find large quantities of the same type of "nurdles" (pellets) on beaches near where spills have occurred; after you've identified the melting point, these can form the majority of the mix that then glues the rest together. Some beaches may contain mostly PET due to large numbers of discarded drink bottles; other beaches will contain a mix.

The majority of plastic waste consists of Type 1 (PET), 2 (HDPE), and 4 (LDPE) plastics. Wherever possible, avoid polystyrene and PVC, as they emit toxic fumes. The nurdles are all thermoplastics, which means they can be remelted. Small plastic fragments found in the top ocean layer are most often HDPE, LDPE, and PP, as they are less dense than sea water and float. However, even if you find thermosetting plastics (which do not melt), these will still form an aggregate within the melted mass.

You will need:

Materials

_Thick tin foil

_Glass fiber roofing insulation

_Crushed charcoal (for best results use perforated charcoal from an old water filter)

_One scrap aluminum L section, approx. 2 x 2 x 15in

_Two steel or stone sheets (for best results use polished stone scraps from kitchen countertops, sink cutouts or leftover floor tiles)

_Wax for mold release (beeswax or automobile polish)

_Three long screws, approx. 3in

_One or two small nuts and bolts

Tools

_Camping stove

_Food tin

_Steel kitchen pan with lid

_Cooking thermometer

_Metal scraper

_Hacksaw

_Drill and metal bits

_Screwdriver

For collecting

_Two buckets

_Kitchen or fine garden sieve

_Dustpan and brush

_Big bag

_Rubber gloves

1

Collection

_Collecting washed-up plastic on the beach is the easiest way to get sea plastic. It also prevents this plastic from returning to the sea to harm marine life. Visit beaches during low tides for deposited materials.

_A dustpan and brush are effective for collecting nurdles. These are often found deposited in lines below the main strand line of heavier materials such as seaweed. If sand is flat and damp, then nurdles can be swept off the surface without collecting the sand. Where sand is collected, separate the sand and plastic by sinking it in a bucket of water and scooping out the floating plastic with a sieve.

_Sort the plastic using the chart to the right. Separate PET from LDPE, HDPE, and PP, which share similar melting points. Dispose of any PVC or polystyrene. Small plastic pieces and nurdles are difficult to identify, but if your averages are correct with the large items, the mix will work well.

_The plastic should all be broken into pieces around ½ x ½ in. This can be done by hand or in a kitchen food processor. Add some water to the mix when using the processor to prevent the plastic from melting around the blades.

_Remember to dry the plastic before melting.

1	2	3	4	5	6
polyethylene terephthalate	high-density polyethylene	polyvinyl chloride	low-density polyethylene	polypropylene	polystyrene
soda bottles, mineral water, fruit juice containers, and cooking oil bottles	containers for milk, cleaning agents, laundry detergents, bleaching agents, shampoo, dishwashing and shower soaps	trays for candy and fruit, plastic packaging (bubble foil), and foils used to wrap foodstuffs	crushed bottles, shopping bags, highly-resistant sacks, and most wrappings	furniture, luggage, and toys, as well as bumpers, lining, and external borders of automobiles	toys, hard packaging, refrigerator trays, cosmetic bags, costume jewelry, audio cassettes, CD cases, vending cups
480°F–500°F **Safe**	Around 250°F **Safe**	210°F–500°F **Toxic**	230°F–320°F **Safe**	260°F–340°F **Safe**	Around 460°F **Toxic**

2

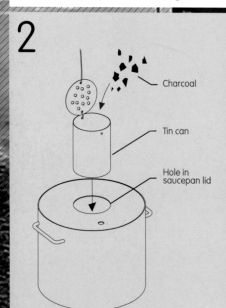

Charcoal

Tin can

Hole in saucepan lid

Furnace

_Drill holes in the lid and the base of the can, and two holes on its sides.

_Thread wire through the lid and tin to form a hinge.

_Break up the charcoal into the smallest possible pieces for better fume absorption, and fill the can.

_Drill a hole in the saucepan lid large enough to take the can and insert the can into the lid.

3

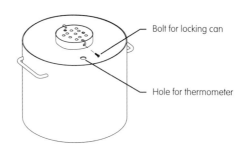

Bolt for locking can

Hole for thermometer

Furnace

_Bolt the can to keep it from falling all the way through the lid.

_Insulate the pan and lid with glass fiber roofing insulation and wrap with tin foil. Do not insulate the base of the pan.

_Check the pan when the temperature reaches around 360°F. If the mix is still hard, turn the heat up to 480°F, checking at intervals to see if the mix is molten. As soon as it is molten enough to form a doughy ball in the pan when stirred, it is ready to use.

_Don't worry if some of the plastic pieces aren't fully melted—as long as the majority are, they will form a colorful aggregate within the material. Be careful not to leave the mixture too long, or the plastic will begin to burn and create more toxic smoke.

_You need to decide whether your plastic mix is largely Type 2, 4, and 5 or Type 1. In most cases it's best to make a mix that mostly consists of Type 2, 4, and 5, which melt in the range of 230–340°C, and use the Type 1 (melts at 480°F) as an aggregate.

_If melting mainly Type 1 (PET), the plastics with a lower melting temperature can be added when the mix is molten and the stove turned off just before filling the mold.

_To make a stool, it's recommended that you heat around three batches of plastic separately, filling the pan each time about a third full. Adding too much in one go will make it difficult to achieve an even temperature throughout the mix.

_An improvised windshield may be required for your furnace to reach higher temperatures.

4

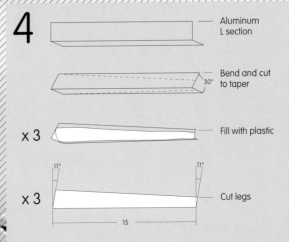

Aluminum
L section

Bend and cut
to taper

30°

x 3

Fill with plastic

x 3

11°   11°

Cut legs

15

Legs
_Take the scrap aluminum L section and bend it to form a
30-degree angle. Taper the sides by cutting the angle at a taper.
_Polish the leg mold with a cloth, and preheat the mold over the
gas stove.
_Use a metal scraper to scoop plastic into the mold, overfilling it
slightly. Press the full leg mold upside down against the flat surface
(stone or steel sheet) until the metal sides are flat against the
surface and the excess plastic squeezes from either side.
Cut off the excess with the metal scraper and return it to the pot
for reuse.
_Submerge the mold in cold water—this speeds up the curing
process and causes the plastic to shrink from the sides of the
mold, enabling easy release.
_Repeat the casting process for the other two legs.
_Cut each leg at top and bottom at an 11-degree angle, as shown.

5

Seat
_A large blob of molten plastic
forms the seat. Pour enough
molten plastic to form a seat of
12in diameter on to a 18 x 18in
granite or marble scrap. Sandwich
the plastic between this and a
second 18 x 18in piece of stone.
Preheat the surface of the stone
so that the plastic stays in a molten
state when pouring, which will result
in a smoother finish.
_You can also use a sheet of smooth
metal instead of stone. Lubricate it
with oil or wax to prevent the plastic
sticking to it.

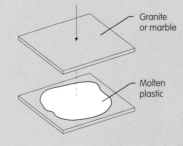

Granite
or marble

Molten
plastic

6

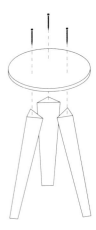

Assembly
_Mark out an equilateral triangle on
the base of the stool where the legs
are to be positioned. Drill holes and
screw in the legs with the screws.
If required, use some of the leftover
melted plastic to weld the legs to the
base of the seat to add strength and
prevent them from twisting.

7

_Take a seat and enjoy!

CHAIR

CHRIS RUCKER OF RUCKERCORP

Chris Rucker made his basic chair in 2001. It was the first truly functional piece he had managed to create after experimenting with oriented strand board (OSB) in various ways, and it became the building block for the rest of his OSB furniture.

Rucker has always been interested in using lesser materials, and pushing them beyond their intended purposes. He is also drawn to materials that are designed to imitate other lesser materials—in this case, OSB as a cheaper version of plywood—and the process of taking a fake of a fake and elevating it to the point where it becomes the "real thing." Aesthetically Rucker was inspired by the sparseness and rigid simplicity of Donald Judd's work, as well as Jasper Morrison's Plywood Chair, and this has been his default approach ever since. "I've made fifteen [other] versions of this chair—curved back, tapered legs, taller, shorter ... they have succeeded at times, and not at others, but I'm not sure they've ever surpassed it."

You will need:

Materials

_One 4 x 8ft sheet of ¾in OSB, or other ¾in sheet material

_Glue

_Brad nails

_Moving blanket

Tools

_Circular saw (a left-tilt table saw; a right-tilt can also be used, but left is easier)

_Nail gun

_Jigsaw

_Router, ⅜in-radius flush trim bit, top or bottom bearing

_Six 18–20in clamps

_Sixteen 3–4in C clamps

_Scissors

_Sewing machine

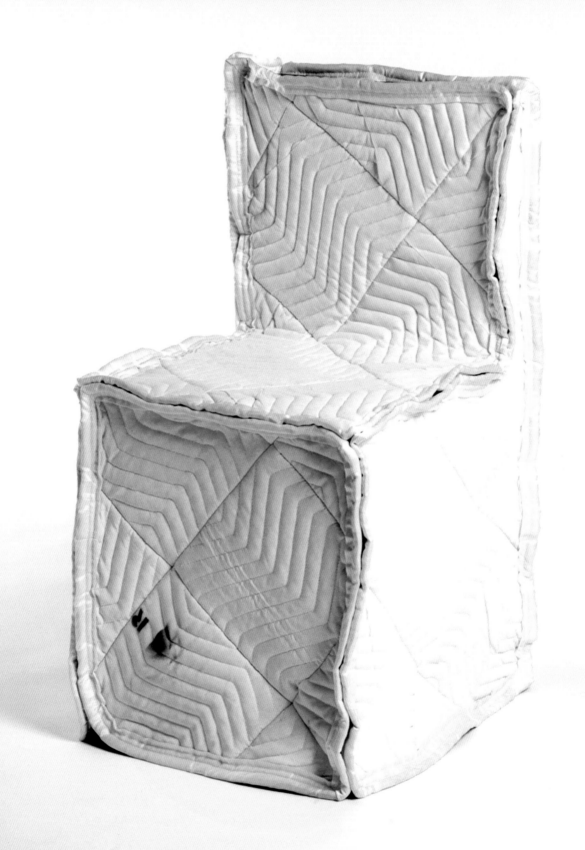

1

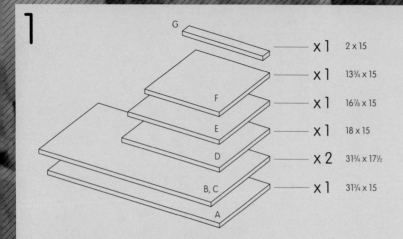

G	× 1	2 × 15
	× 1	13¾ × 15
F	× 1	16⅞ × 15
E	× 1	18 × 15
D	× 2	31¾ × 17½
B, C	× 1	31¾ × 15
A		

_Cut the sheet of of OSB into thirds across the 8ft length, ending up with three identical pieces, measuring 32 × 48in. Cut out the following seven chair parts from the three OSB pieces:
_One × 31¾ × 15in (part A)
_Two × 31¾ × 17½in (parts B and C)
_One × 18 × 15in (part D)
_One × 16⅞ × 15in (part E)
_One × 13¾ × 15in (part F)
_One × 2 × 15in (part G)

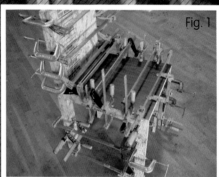

Fig. 1

2

_Clamp the pieces to a piece of scrap material and use the circular saw to cut out the chair parts from the OSB following the dimensions above. Or, if you are as skilled as Chris Rucker, you can use a table saw and raise the blade through the OSB in order to cut the various chair parts.
_Cut a miter of 45 degrees on the edges highlighted right in gray.
_Cut a ⅛in dado (¾in-wide channel) into part A, as shown. The location of the channel is critical as it joins the seat and establishes the seat height.
_Use the jigsaw to help cut out the tighter corners on part E and the material between the legs, leaving enough material to make a ⅜in radius on the inside corners with the router.
_Use a router with a ⅜in radius flush trim bit and round.

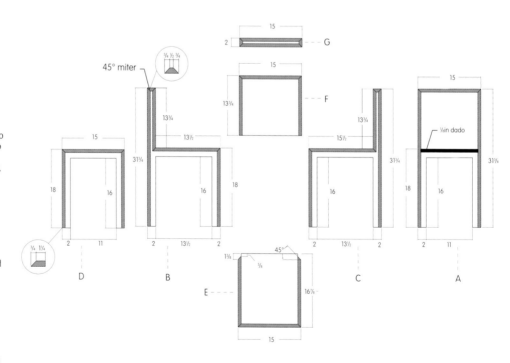

3

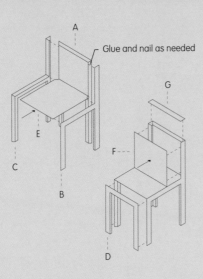

Glue and nail as needed

A
G
E
C
B
F
D

_Start by gluing the seat (part E) to the back (part A) via the dado channel. Fit them together and use a nail gun to shoot a couple of nails in from the back.
_Glue and nail the side legs (parts B and C) to the chair.
_Glue and nail the front legs (part D), seat back (part F), and top piece (part G) to finish off the assembly.
_Clamp the chair across its width above the legs in a few places, and put two clamps from the back to the front over the 17½in dimension with an adjacent clamp out at the front of the seat. Then with as many 3–4in C clamps, clamp the miters of all the legs; four clamps per leg is best, as shown in Fig. 1.

4

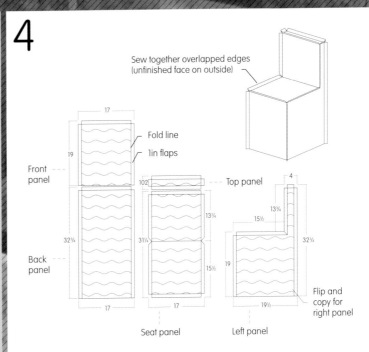

Sew together overlapped edges
(unfinished face on outside)

Front panel
Back panel
17
19
32¾
17
Fold line
1in flaps
Top panel
102
31¼
13¼
15½
17
Seat panel
4
13¼
15½
19
32¾
19½
Left panel
Flip and copy for right panel

_Use scissors to cut the moving blanket into chair cover parts following the dimensions above; 1in flaps have been added to the three sides that don't touch the floor for attaching to each adjacent piece.
_Once all the pieces are cut out, pin the cover on to the chair, making sure the unfinished side of the cover is facing outward. You'll have an extra couple of centimeters of material at every seam, so account for that when you're pinning it. Tailor the cover a little bit and trim any seams if necessary.
_Take the pinned cover off the chair and sew/bind all the seams.

5

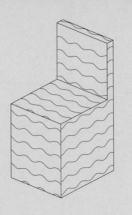

_Flip the sewn cover inside out (finished side and seams facing outward) and place it on the chair. The cover should fit the chair snugly.
_Take a seat and enjoy!

See also p.106 for Chris Rucker's Quilt.

LEFTOVERS

KLEMENS SCHILLINGER

The Leftovers stools are simple pieces that are formed by using a conventional builder's bucket as the mold for the seating surface. Wooden scrap pieces are clamped into the bucket. Concrete is then poured into the void. Within a few hours the hardened concrete bonds in the wooden legs and the stool is ready for use.

The idea for the stools was derived from using a reversed bucket as a seat as well as often finding leftover plaster and other hardened casting materials in the bottom of a builder's bucket after a day in the workshop. The simple materials used capture the spirit and the aesthetics of the informal design language. The project also suggests the use of informal molds for other products (lampshades, vessels, etc.) as quick and cheap alternatives to the laborious formal mold-making process.

You will need:

Materials

_Concrete mix

_Three wooden planks
 (approximately 40cm)

Tools

_Handsaw

_3 G clamps

_2 builder's buckets

_Stanley knife

_Brown packaging tape

1

16

x 3

Stool legs
_Cut the wooden planks into three equally long parts.
Approximately 16in is a conventional stool height.
_Cut a little groove in each leg. This will ensure the leg
is captured in the concrete.
_Seal the end of the planks that will go into the concrete
with brown packaging tape (this prevents the wood from
absorbing the water, which might make it expand and
crack the concrete).

2

_Insert the three stool legs into an
empty bucket.
_Clamp the legs with a spacer
(approximately ½–1in thick) onto the
wall of the bucket (shown in Fig. 1).
_Make sure the legs do not touch the
bottom of the bucket and the legs
are equally spaced in the bucket.
Optionally, you can reinforce the
concrete by wrapping wire around
the legs when already clamped
into the bucket.

3

_Take the second bucket and start
mixing the concrete thoroughly.
Once the concrete has been mixed
(Fig. 2), start pouring it into the void
of the prepared bucket (shown in
Fig. 3) with the clamped wood legs,
then shake the bucket for a few
seconds to even out the liquid mix.
Tip: You can use premixed concrete
from the DIY store, or if you prefer to
mix your own concrete, use one part
cement to one part sand then add
water and mix to a consistency that
is neither too dry nor too soupy.
_You can also add some wood glue
to the mix to strengthen the mixture.

Fig. 1

Fig. 2

Fig. 3

4

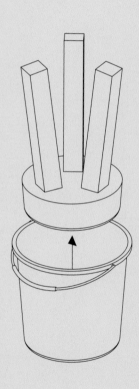

_Wait for the concrete to cure.
Depending on the concrete, this can
take up to 24 hours.
_Remove the stool from the mold.
Cut away any visible brown tape
from the underside of the concrete
with a utility knife.

5

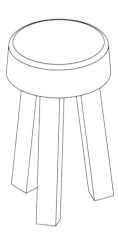

_Take a seat and enjoy!

4.
LIGHTING

Utility has never looked so good! The designers in this section are well versed in bringing standard materials into a new light. Two of the designs rethink standard fixtures and bulbs that you would normally see in industrial applications, while two others build on the way we interact with light. Dim(Some) does just that, allowing the user not only to dim the amount of light, but, through Arduino coding, the intensity of light too, while 45 Kilo have created a light that can be easily adjusted to shine where you need it. Sara Ebert gives the cage light a new spin and skin, adding a sleeve of rubber to create multiple playful configurations. Growing out of a simple block of wood, the U-shaped bulb of the T8 light appears to draw its shape into the air. Regardless of your preference, this round-up of lights will certainly have you flipping switches.

CONTOUR LAMP

SARA EBERT

Inspired by the properties of industrial heat shrink tubing, these lamps were created by forming large-diameter tubing over the wire lightbulb guards often used on construction sites. The tubing becomes extremely taut, accentuating the contours of the steel forms and creating a shade for the bulb.

This project was conceived in response to the brief put forth by the American Design Club for their show "Raw + Unfiltered." The premise of the show was to showcase designs that highlighted a material or process in its most natural, unfiltered state.

Sara is based in the US so we have reproduced her wiring instructions overleaf but if you live outside of the US, you will need to adapt the wiring to local specifications.

You will need:

Materials

The following can be found at Grand Brass:

_One standard single socket (SO10045C)

_10in black 18/3 SVT cord (WI183SVTBL)

_One stress reliever terminal (BG500BLK)

_Plug (PL183BL)

_Heat shrink tube (HS2-600), at least 6in (available from BuyHeatShrink)

_Light cages (available at various hardware outlets; this one can be found on Amazon)

Tools

_Scissors

_Standard screwdriver

_Precision micro screwdriver

_Wire stripper

_Utility knife

_Metal ruler

_Heat gun

1

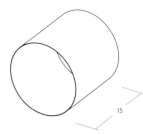

15

_Cut 6in of heat shrink tubing. The
tubing arrives in a flattened state
and can easily be cut using a metal
ruler and utility knife.

2

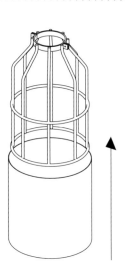

_Slide the tubing over the top of the cage.
_Apply heat to the tubing using
the heat gun, constantly moving
around the cage to ensure an even,
consistent shrinkage.

3

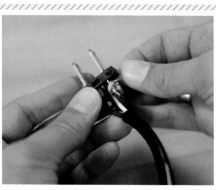

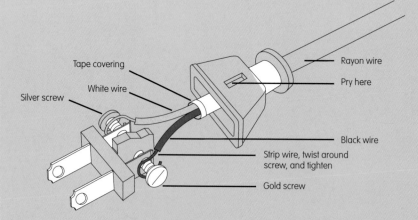

Tape covering

White wire

Silver screw

Rayon wire

Pry here

Black wire

Strip wire, twist around
screw, and tighten

Gold screw

Wiring the plug
_Use a screwdriver to prize the rubber cover off the plug interior.
_Tape the rayon covering to keep it clean.
_Strip the wires, twist them around the screws, and tighten the screws down
(black wire to gold screw, white wire to silver screw).
_Push the rubber cover back in place.

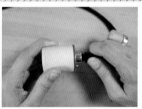

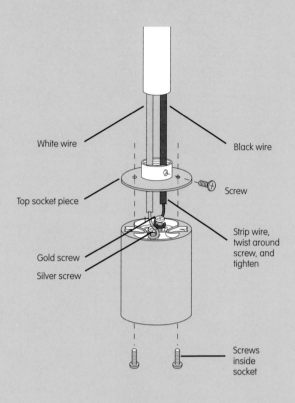

White wire

Black wire

Top socket piece

Screw

Gold screw

Silver screw

Strip wire,
twist around
screw, and
tighten

...ire to the gold
...ite wire to the

...s reliever terminal
... reliever parts
... socket are slid
...re completing the
...ections).
... socket down and
... Slide the lower
...eliever terminal
...t into the socket.
... terminal down
...w it into place over

Screws
inside
socket

5

Screw

_Place the socket into the ring on the top of
the light cage.
_Hold it in place and screw both sides,
clamping the socket in place (move it back
and forth between the two screws as the
cage is tightened to ensure even clamping).
_Add your lightbulb.

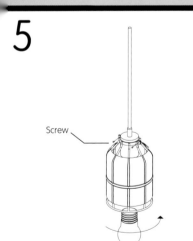

6

_Hang and enjoy!

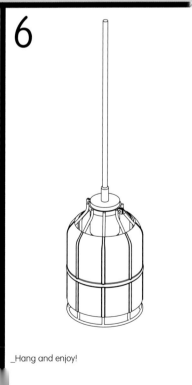

T8

SARAH PEASE

The T8, little brother of the T12, is an exploration in form and material. This light is designed from readily available, standard parts, combined with solid black walnut and a soft fabric cord.

This project was an experiment using premade parts—most of which can be found in any hardware store. The entire piece is constructed with magnets and press-fit components, so is easily disassembled/reassembled. The base consists of two pieces of wood held together by magnets. These design features also allow for simple assembly and easy access for troubleshooting—perfect for an ambitious DIYer. The design itself is easily customizable, too; changes to the wood or metal finishing can produce an end result with its own unique aesthetic.

Once the T8 U-bulb is inserted into the base, the light comes to life. Its overly luminous fluorescent light, set against the polished, elegant materials, creates new associations for an industrial product.

You will need:

Materials

_Four neodymium magnets, ½in diameter

_One toggle switch

_Lamp cord, 8ft long

_One plug

_One fluorescent lighting kit or comparable materials (ballast, wires, etc.)

_One T8 fluorescent U-bend lightbulb with 6in leg spacing

_Wire nuts

_Solder

_Electrical tape

_Epoxy

_Aluminum tubing (large enough for the lightbulb to fit into, 1¼in diameter)

_Wood of choice

_Wood finish

Tools

_Wire strippers/cutters

_Flathead screwdriver

_Soldering iron

_Table saw

_Hand router

_Drill, with bits to match the size of the metal tubing, magnets, and toggle switch

_Sandpaper

_Safety equipment

1

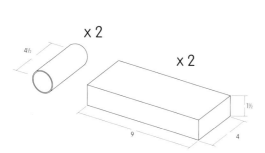

_Cut the metal tubing into two lengths
of 4½in.
_Cut the wood into two pieces
measuring 4 x 9 x 1½in.

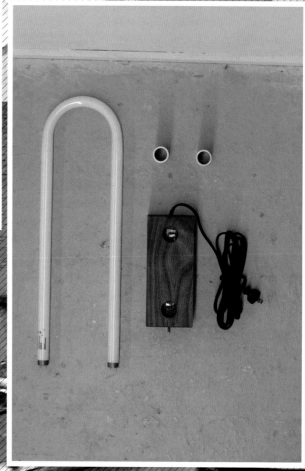

2

_In both pieces of wood, drill aligning shallow holes in all
four corners of one of the wider faces. (These should be
the depth of your magnets, so that when they are glued
in they sit flush with the top of the wood.)
_Use the router to cut out a pocket in the middle section.
The resulting hole should be a rectangle that measures
1 x 8½ x 1½in deep. This piece will be the bottom of the
light (part A).
_Drill a hole in the center on both ends of the bottom
piece. One hole should fit the toggle switch, and the
other hole should fit the lamp cord.
_Take the other piece of wood, which is the top (part B),
and drill two larger holes with diameters that correspond
to the metal tubing (1¼in). The holes should be 6in apart,
center to center.
_Cut two scrap pieces the width of the pocket (1in) and 3in
long (part C).

Top view

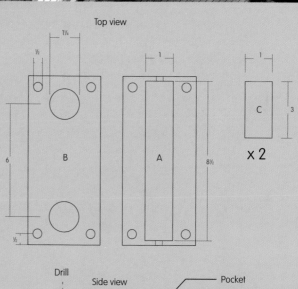

Drill

Side view

Pocket

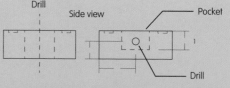

Drill

3

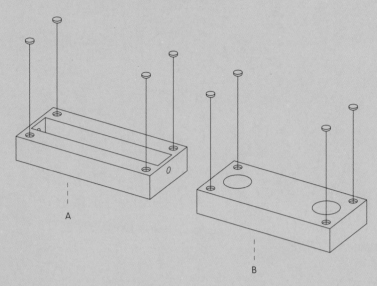

A

B

_Glue the magnets into the holes using epoxy so that the pieces of wood will snap together to make one larger piece, measuring 4 x 9 x 3in. Make sure that the magnets are aligned with their counterparts, otherwise they will repel and the wood will not stick together.

4

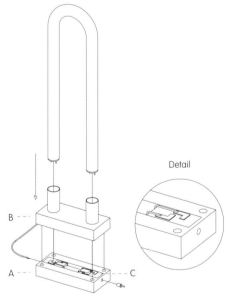

Detail

B

A ---- C

_Place the ballast inside the pocket of part A.
_Place the two scrap pieces of wood (parts C) on top of the ballast, using epoxy to glue the wires down so that the copper contact will line up with each pin of the T8 bulb.
_Snap the two pieces of wood together and insert the metal tubes into the two holes.
_If there is a stretcher bar connecting the bottom of the U-bulb, remove it.

5

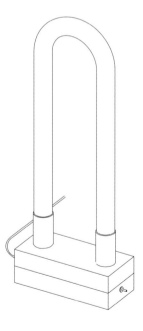

_Insert the lightbulb into the metal tubes, turn on, and enjoy!

MOKKA LIGHT

45 KILO

The Mokka Light is simply put together, using a classical geometric lampshade made from passe-partout (framing board), some standard copper piping, and some electrical wire. Assembling these parts creates a certain lightness—the lamp seems to be floating in the room.

The adjustable ceiling installation also allows the lamp to be placed where it is needed. By pulling the wire through the rod, the height of the shade can easily be changed.

You will need:

Materials

_Black-and-white passe-partout cardboard, 28 x 40in

_Roll of adhesive aluminum tape, width ¾in

_Lightbulb

_Bulb holder

_Electrical wire, 200in long, diameter not more than ⅜in

_Copper pipe, 100in long, ⅜in diameter

_Ceiling hook, at least ½in diameter

Tools

_Cutter

_Scissors

_Steel ruler

_Cutting mat

1

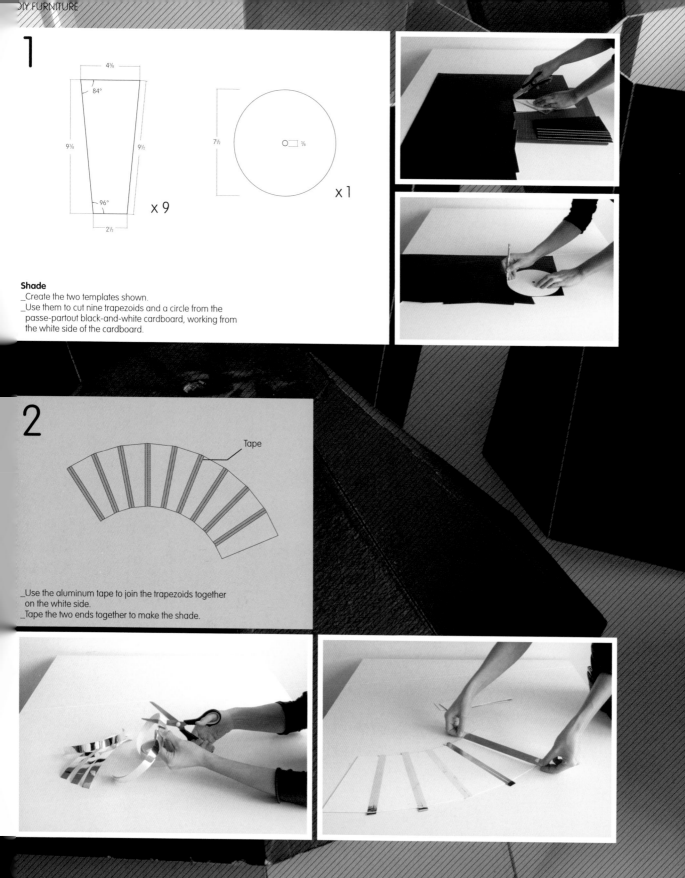

Shade

_Create the two templates shown.
_Use them to cut nine trapezoids and a circle from the passe-partout black-and-white cardboard, working from the white side of the cardboard.

2

Tape

_Use the aluminum tape to join the trapezoids together on the white side.
_Tape the two ends together to make the shade.

3

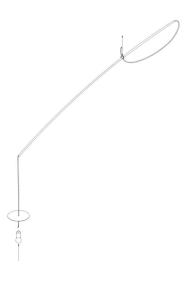

Pivot arm
_Cut the copper pipe to 100in and pull the cable through it.
_Make sure the fuse for the ceiling outlet is turned off.
_Hang the pipe on the ceiling hook next to the outlet and
 connect the cables.
_Mount the bulb holder with the cardboard circle at the other
 end of the cable.

4

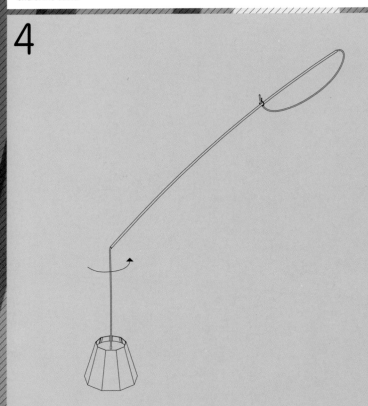

_Hang the shade over the circle and you're done.
_Now you can circle the light around the room and
 change the height of the shade by pulling the cable to
 one side or the other. Enjoy!

DIM(SOME) CHANDELIER

BRENDAN KEIM

This chandelier explores how light can grow both in quantity and intensity, controlled through the familiar interface of dimmer knobs. The user can create more light by turning bulbs on or off with one knob (quantity), while a second knob adjusts the brightness of the light emitted from each bulb (intensity). Intensity can also be manipulated at each level of quantity.

The integration of the Arduino platform into Brendan's work is one more way of embracing DIY design. "The whole basis for Arduino is open-source software and hardware. The open-source community surrounding Arduino is rooted in the idea of sharing your ideas with others … not only to show off what you've made to the world, but also to allow others to alter your ideas … either for their own needs and designs, or to enhance and improve what you have made. I don't really consider myself an expert in coding or electronics, but the Arduino platform allows me to make my ideas real. If someone else can make it better or suggest methods for me to make it better, that's great. It's like collective intelligence."

You will need:

Materials

From Grand Brass

_One 2-pronged plug (part A, item # PL183PBK)
_Cloth-wrapped cord, 10ft long (part B)
_One 3-sided cluster body, 1/4F bottom, 1/8F top
  (part C, item # BOLG3)
_Two 3-sided cluster bodies, 1/8F bottom, 1/8F top
  (part D, item # BOLG3X8)
_Two 4-sided cluster bodies, 1/4F bottom, 1/8F top
  (part E, item # BOLG4)
_Three 9in x 1/8 IPS brass pipe stems, threaded both ends
  (part F, item # PIBR09-0X8)
_Three 7in x 1/8 IPS brass pipe stems, threaded both ends
  (part G, item # PIBR07-0X8)
_Two 5in x 1/8 IPS brass pipe stems, threaded both ends
  (part H, item # PIBR05-0X8)
_Three 3in x 1/8 IPS brass pipe stems, threaded both ends
  (part I, item # PIBR03-0X8)
_Five 1in x 1/8 IPS brass pipe stems, threaded both ends (part
  J, item # PIBR01-0X8)
_Four ¾in x 1/8 IPS threaded nipples
  (part K, item # N10-3/4x1/8)
_Eighteen black Edison (E-26) base phenolic sockets
  (part L, item # SO7175B)
_One 14in x 1/4 IPS brass pipe stem, threaded both ends
  (part M, item # PIBR14-0X4)
_One 6in brass canopy, 1in deep
  (part N, item # BAFL06NW)
_One brass loop 1/4 IPS (part O, item # LO103)
_One female rounded brass hook 1/8 IPS
  (part P, item # HK105)

From McMaster-Carr
_Black stranded single conductor wire, 200ft long
  (part Q, item # 7587K133)
_White stranded single conductor wire, 200ft long
  (part R, item # 7587K138)
_Two knurled brass knobs (part S, item # 5125K1)

From most hardware stores
_One Leviton Trimatron 600-watt electro-mechanical push
  dimmer (part T)
_¾in board, 3 x 60in
_¼in board, 24 x 24in
_24 small nails

From Digi-Key
_Twelve solid state relays, 8A (part U, item #425-2403-5-ND)

From RadioShack
_One 10K-ohm linear potentiometer (part V, item # 271-1715)

From Modern Device
_One Arduino board (part W, item # MD0001)
_One wall power adapter, 6V 1A (part X, item # MD0405)
_Eighteen terminal blocks, 2 position (part Y, item # CP0712)
_Housing box (with removable lid). Approximately 9in W x
  15in H x 2½in D (custom box shown).

Tools
_Arduino (software & hardware) w/ computer
_Wire strippers
_Soldering iron
_Diagonal snips
_Screwdrivers—Phillips and flathead, various sizes
_Voltmeter/multimeter
_Saw
_Miter saw
_Router or table saw for grooves
_Drill
_Hammer
_Wood glue

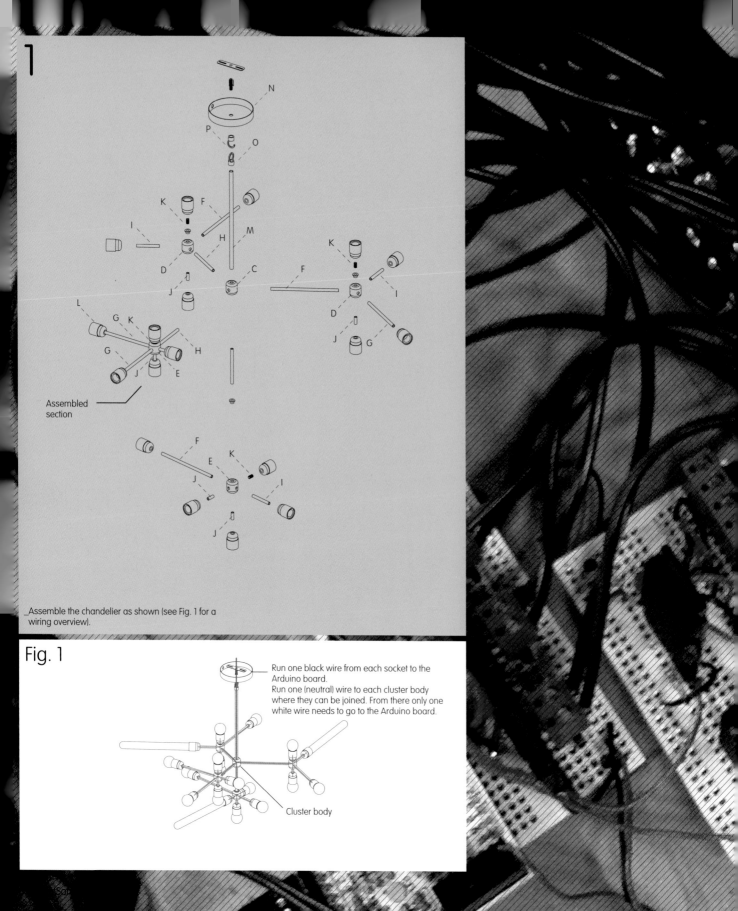

1

N

P

O

K F

I

H M

D C

J

L

G K

G

G H

J E

Assembled
section

F

E K

J I

J

_Assemble the chandelier as shown (see Fig. 1 for a
wiring overview).

Fig. 1

Run one black wire from each socket to the
Arduino board.
Run one (neutral) wire to each cluster body
where they can be joined. From there only one
white wire needs to go to the Arduino board.

Cluster body

2

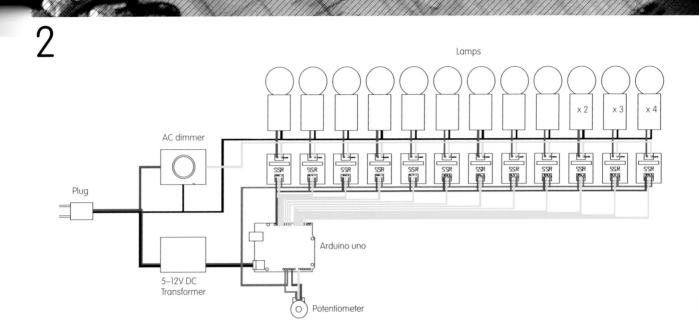

Lamps

x 2 x 3 x 4

AC dimmer

SSR SSR SSR SSR SSR SSR SSR SSR SSR SSR SSR SSR

Plug

Arduino uno

5–12V DC
Transformer

Potentiometer

_Assemble the dimmer board as
 shown.

3

2½   9

2½

8

15

16

Drill

Drill

1

1

_Create a box large enough to house the electronics.
_Use ¾in boards to create the perimeter. Cut to 2½in wide and use a router or table
 saw to notch out ¼ x ¼in on the inside corners.
_Cut to the following lengths and miter the ends:
 Two, 16in long; two, 9in long.
_Use wood glue where they join, and screw or nail them together.
_Drill a hole in the top and bottom boards for your cord.
_Cut two ¼in-thick panels to 15 x 8in. In one of the panels, drill two ¼in holes for
 your knobs approximately 1in from each corner as shown.
_Attach with small nails.

```
/*Dim(Some) Board by Brendan
  Keim. www.brendankeim.com
Read a potentiometer and output
  reading to digital pins.
*/
int potVal = 0;
int potPin = 0;
void setup() {
pinMode(2, OUTPUT);
pinMode(3, OUTPUT);
pinMode(4, OUTPUT);
pinMode(5, OUTPUT);
pinMode(6, OUTPUT);
pinMode(7, OUTPUT);
pinMode(8, OUTPUT);
pinMode(9, OUTPUT);
pinMode(10, OUTPUT);
pinMode(11, OUTPUT);
pinMode(12, OUTPUT);
pinMode(13, OUTPUT);
Serial.begin(9600);
}

void loop() {
potVal = analogRead(A0);
delay(20);
//Serial.println(potVal, DEC);
// delay(300); // short delay to
  keep from sending too much data
  to serial port
potPin = map(potVal,0,1023,0,14);
//Serial.println(potPin, DEC);
//delay(300);
if (potPin == 0)
{
digitalWrite(2, HIGH);
digitalWrite(3, LOW);
digitalWrite(4, LOW);
digitalWrite(5, LOW);
digitalWrite(6, LOW);
digitalWrite(7, LOW);
digitalWrite(8, LOW);
digitalWrite(9, LOW);
digitalWrite(10, LOW);
digitalWrite(11, LOW);
digitalWrite(12, LOW);
digitalWrite(13, LOW);
}
else if (potPin == 1)
{
digitalWrite(2, HIGH);
digitalWrite(3, LOW);
digitalWrite(4, LOW);
digitalWrite(5, LOW);
digitalWrite(6, LOW);
digitalWrite(7, LOW);
digitalWrite(8, LOW);
digitalWrite(9, LOW);
digitalWrite(10, LOW);
digitalWrite(11, LOW);
digitalWrite(12, LOW);
digitalWrite(13, LOW);
}
else if (potPin == 2){
digitalWrite(2, HIGH);
digitalWrite(3, LOW);
digitalWrite(4, LOW);
digitalWrite(5, LOW);
digitalWrite(6, LOW);
digitalWrite(7, LOW);
digitalWrite(8, LOW);
digitalWrite(9, LOW);
digitalWrite(10, LOW);
digitalWrite(11, LOW);
digitalWrite(12, LOW);
digitalWrite(13, LOW);
}
else if (potPin == 3){
digitalWrite(2, HIGH);
digitalWrite(3, HIGH);
digitalWrite(4, LOW);
digitalWrite(5, LOW);
digitalWrite(6, LOW);
digitalWrite(7, LOW);
digitalWrite(8, LOW);
digitalWrite(9, LOW);
digitalWrite(10, LOW);
digitalWrite(11, LOW);
digitalWrite(12, LOW);
digitalWrite(13, LOW);
}
else if (potPin == 4){
digitalWrite(2, HIGH);
digitalWrite(3, HIGH);
digitalWrite(4, HIGH);
digitalWrite(5, LOW);
digitalWrite(6, LOW);
digitalWrite(7, LOW);
digitalWrite(8, LOW);
digitalWrite(9, LOW);
digitalWrite(10, LOW);
digitalWrite(11, LOW);
digitalWrite(12, LOW);
digitalWrite(13, LOW);
}
else if (potPin == 5){
digitalWrite(2, HIGH);
digitalWrite(3, HIGH);
digitalWrite(4, HIGH);
digitalWrite(5, HIGH);
digitalWrite(6, LOW);
digitalWrite(7, LOW);
digitalWrite(8, LOW);
digitalWrite(9, LOW);
digitalWrite(10, LOW);
digitalWrite(11, LOW);
digitalWrite(12, LOW);
digitalWrite(13, LOW);
}
else if (potPin == 6){
digitalWrite(2, HIGH);
digitalWrite(3, HIGH);
digitalWrite(4, HIGH);
digitalWrite(5, HIGH);
digitalWrite(6, HIGH);
digitalWrite(7, LOW);
digitalWrite(8, LOW);
digitalWrite(9, LOW);
digitalWrite(10, LOW);
digitalWrite(11, LOW);
digitalWrite(12, LOW);
digitalWrite(13, LOW);
}
else if (potPin == 7){
digitalWrite(2, HIGH);
digitalWrite(3, HIGH);
digitalWrite(4, HIGH);
digitalWrite(5, HIGH);
digitalWrite(6, HIGH);
digitalWrite(7, HIGH);
digitalWrite(8, LOW);
digitalWrite(9, LOW);
digitalWrite(10, LOW);
digitalWrite(11, LOW);
digitalWrite(12, LOW);
digitalWrite(13, LOW);
}
else if (potPin == 8){
digitalWrite(2, HIGH);
digitalWrite(3, HIGH);
digitalWrite(4, HIGH);
digitalWrite(5, HIGH);
digitalWrite(6, HIGH);
digitalWrite(7, HIGH);
digitalWrite(8, HIGH);
digitalWrite(9, LOW);
digitalWrite(10, LOW);
digitalWrite(11, LOW);
digitalWrite(12, LOW);
digitalWrite(13, LOW);
}
else if (potPin == 9){
digitalWrite(2, HIGH);
digitalWrite(3, HIGH);
digitalWrite(4, HIGH);
digitalWrite(5, HIGH);
digitalWrite(6, HIGH);
digitalWrite(7, HIGH);
digitalWrite(8, HIGH);
digitalWrite(9, HIGH);
digitalWrite(10, LOW);
digitalWrite(11, LOW);
digitalWrite(12, LOW);
digitalWrite(13, LOW);
}
else if (potPin == 10){
digitalWrite(2, HIGH);
digitalWrite(3, HIGH);
digitalWrite(4, HIGH);
digitalWrite(5, HIGH);
digitalWrite(6, HIGH);
digitalWrite(7, HIGH);
digitalWrite(8, HIGH);
digitalWrite(9, HIGH);
digitalWrite(10, HIGH);
digitalWrite(11, LOW);
digitalWrite(12, LOW);
digitalWrite(13, LOW);
}
else if (potPin == 11){
digitalWrite(2, HIGH);
digitalWrite(3, HIGH);
digitalWrite(4, HIGH);
digitalWrite(5, HIGH);
digitalWrite(6, HIGH);
digitalWrite(7, HIGH);
digitalWrite(8, HIGH);
digitalWrite(9, HIGH);
digitalWrite(10, HIGH);
digitalWrite(11, HIGH);
digitalWrite(12, LOW);
digitalWrite(13, LOW);
}
else if (potPin == 12){
digitalWrite(2, HIGH);
digitalWrite(3, HIGH);
digitalWrite(4, HIGH);
digitalWrite(5, HIGH);
digitalWrite(6, HIGH);
digitalWrite(7, HIGH);
digitalWrite(8, HIGH);
digitalWrite(9, HIGH);
digitalWrite(10, HIGH);
digitalWrite(11, HIGH);
digitalWrite(12, HIGH);
digitalWrite(13, LOW);
}
else if (potPin == 13){
digitalWrite(2, HIGH);
digitalWrite(3, HIGH);
digitalWrite(4, HIGH);
digitalWrite(5, HIGH);
digitalWrite(6, HIGH);
digitalWrite(7, HIGH);
digitalWrite(8, HIGH);
digitalWrite(9, HIGH);
digitalWrite(10, HIGH);
digitalWrite(11, HIGH);
digitalWrite(12, HIGH);
digitalWrite(13, HIGH);
}
else if (potPin == 14){
digitalWrite(2, HIGH);
digitalWrite(3, HIGH);
digitalWrite(4, HIGH);
digitalWrite(5, HIGH);
digitalWrite(6, HIGH);
digitalWrite(7, HIGH);
digitalWrite(8, HIGH);
digitalWrite(9, HIGH);
digitalWrite(10, HIGH);
digitalWrite(11, HIGH);
digitalWrite(12, HIGH);
digitalWrite(13, HIGH);
}
}
```

_Upload custom code to Arduino.
Found at: www.brendankeim.com/DIM-SOME-CHANDELIER

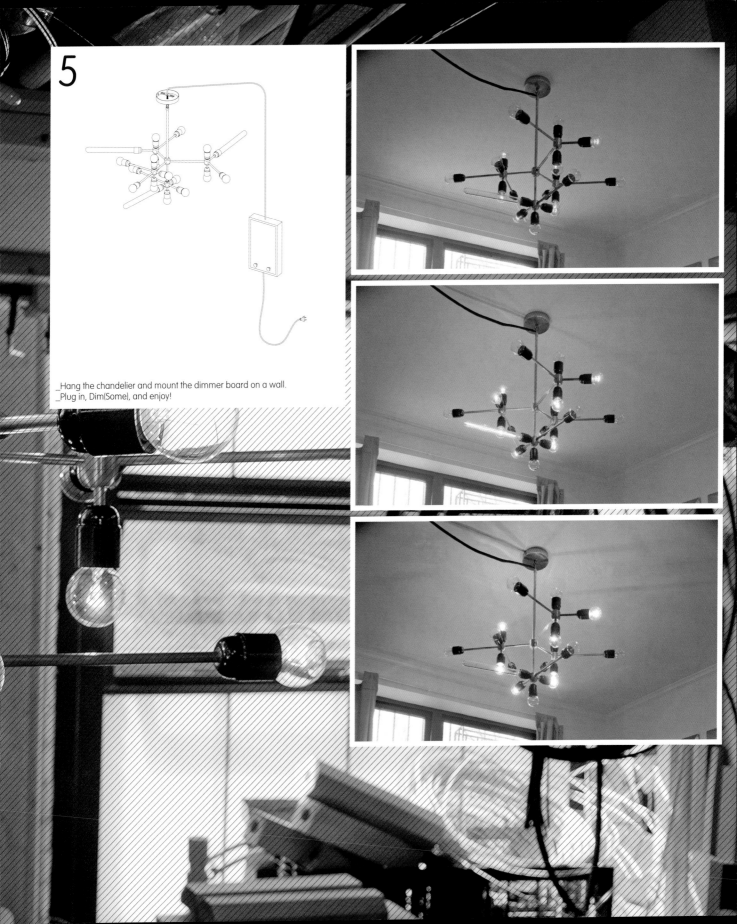

5

_Hang the chandelier and mount the dimmer board on a wall.
_Plug in, Dim(Some), and enjoy!

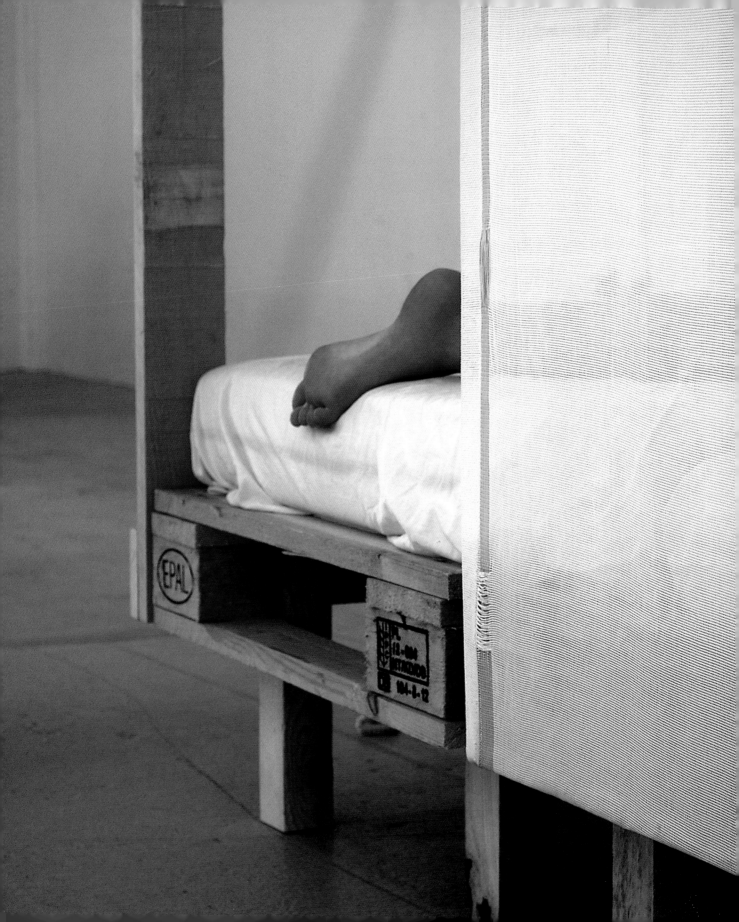

5.
BEDROOM

Closets are overrated. They are usually cramped, dark spaces that do a better job of hiding junk than functioning as a place from which to select your daily digs. From storage that displays to a quilt that once moved, this selection of designs will get you inspired at the start of your day. If you need a room within a room, Retreat will give you privacy while you dream up your next project. Wake up and drop down the incorporated desk and get to work making Ruckercorp's Quilt from moving blankets. We provide you with the bones for creating this eye-popping piece of modernism so that you can make it your own. Display your most cherished fashion-forward item prominently in the A.O.CMS Glass Cabinet, originally designed for a store in Sweden to showcase their wares. Love Aesthetics' take on a clothing rack is not only functional but also a beautiful example of minimalism. The Lesser Dresser, a monolith of OSB, also shows off your belongings. The top drawer is designed to house your collection of accessories, which are visible through a slightly reflective glass top that also functions as a mirror.

CLOTHING RACK

LOVE AESTHETICS

This is a new version of the standard clothing rail, made out of basic plumbing parts. The design has been kept as easy and uncomplicated as possible—it is essentially just a frame that leans against the wall.

The weight of the clothes pushes the rack against the wall and makes it sturdy, while the simplicity of the design also makes it really easy to deconstruct and move around.

1

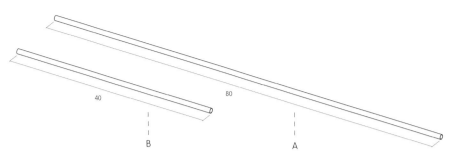

40   80

B   A

Cut the ⅞in-diameter plumbing tube to the following lengths:
_Two x 80in (part A)
_Two x 40in (part B)

2

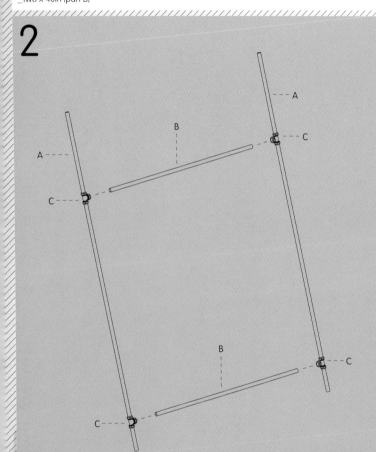

A
B
C
A
C
C
B
C

Fig. 1

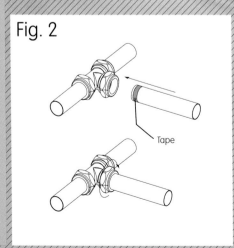

Fig. 2

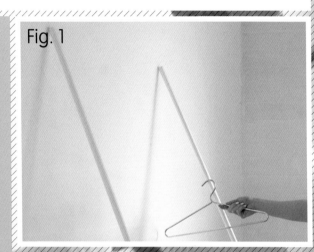

Tape

_Put the long tubes against the wall at an incline, with the
 bottom approximately 30in away from the wall.
_Position a hanger at a height where it doesn't touch the
 wall and mark this spot on the tube (see Fig. 1). This is
 where the horizontal tube (part B) will be located.
_Put a piece of strong tape around the ends of the
 horizontal tubes (parts B) before inserting into three-way
 joints (parts C) to prevent them from sliding.
_Once all four joints have been placed, finish assembling
 the rack by connecting the long tubes with the short
 horizontal ones in between (see Fig. 2).

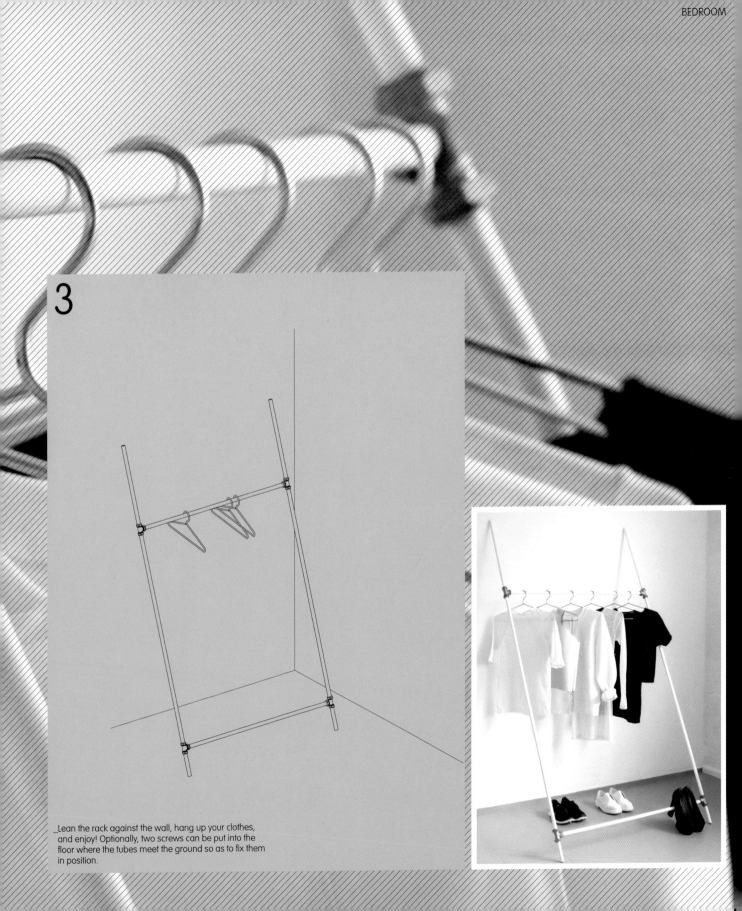

3

_Lean the rack against the wall, hang up your clothes, and enjoy! Optionally, two screws can be put into the floor where the tubes meet the ground so as to fix them in position.

OSBEAUTIFUL LESSER DRESSER

CHRISTOPHER STUART

Oriented strand board (OSB)—also referred to as chipboard, shit board, wafer board, pancake board, sterling board, exterior board, smartply, and "that crappy stuff that gives you bad splinters"—is a subpar sheet commonly used for underflooring, roofing, decking, and crates. On the woodworker's desired list of materials, it rates even lower than plywood.

Christopher Stuart chose to use this material, not only because it is so rarely used for furniture but also because it was potentially so well suited to a dresser form—a crate, just like a dresser, tends to inspire curiosity about what's inside. To incorporate this sense of curiosity, Stuart removed all visible hardware from the outside, allowing the dresser to feel like one solid object.

The usual solid top of a dresser is replaced here with reflective bronze glass—it is somewhat see-through, but requires the effort of leaning over, which adds a bit of intrigue. Opening the top drawer reveals corrugated foam, which could cradle precious collectables like watches or jewelry.

Historical cabinet-making techniques were used for this piece—matched "grain" and rough drawer sides—alongside high-end ball-bearing slide hardware, creating an odd pairing of low- and high-brow. It is this pairing that elevates the OSB to another level and earns it the nickname, OSBeautiful.

You will need:

Materials

_Ten 16in-long ball-bearing slides

_One piece of tempered reflective bronze glass

_Four sheets of OSB, ¾ x 95 x 48in

_Two sheets of OSB, ½ x 95 x 48in

_Two aluminum angles, ½ x ½ x 60in

_Drywall screws, ½in long

_Drywall screws, 1¾in long

_Drywall screws, 2½in long

_Finish nails, 1¼in long

_Wood glue

Tools

_Drill

_Drill bit for metal, ⅛in diameter

_Metal hacksaw

_Saw

_Hammer

_Long-bladed utility knife

1

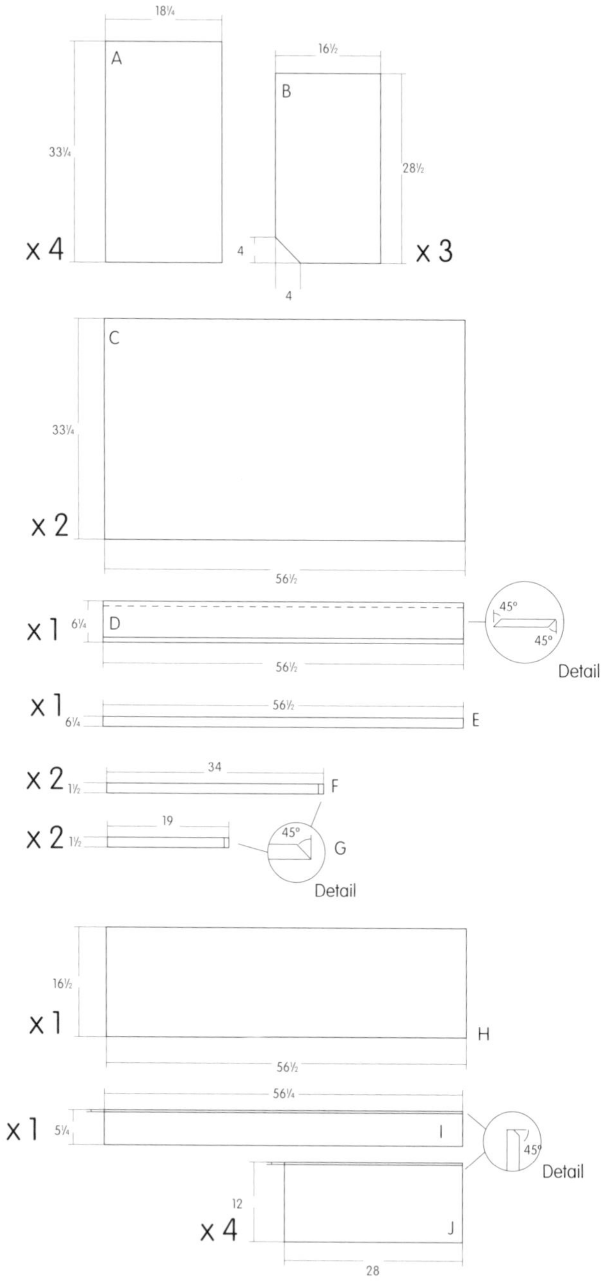
18¼
A
33¼
x 4
16½
B
28½
4
4
x 3
C
33¼
x 2
56½
x 1
6¼
D
56½
45°
45°
Detail
x 1
56½
6¼
E
x 2
34
1½
F
x 2
19
1½
45°
G
Detail
16½
x 1
H
56½
56¼
x 1
5¼
I
45°
Detail
12
x 4
J
28

Cut the ¾in OSB to the following sizes:
_Four x 18¼ x 33¼in (part A)
_Three x 16½ x 28½in with 4in diagonal corner (part B)
_Two x 56½ x 33¼in (part C)
_One x 56½ x 6¼in with mitered sides, see detail (part D)
_One x 56½ x 1½in (part E)
_Two x 34 x 1½in with mitered end, see detail (part F)
_Two x 19 x 1½in with mitered end, see detail (part G)
_One x 56½ x 16½in (part H)
_One x 56¼ x 5¼mm with beveled edge, see detail (part I)
_Four x 28 x 12in with beveled edge, see detail (part J)

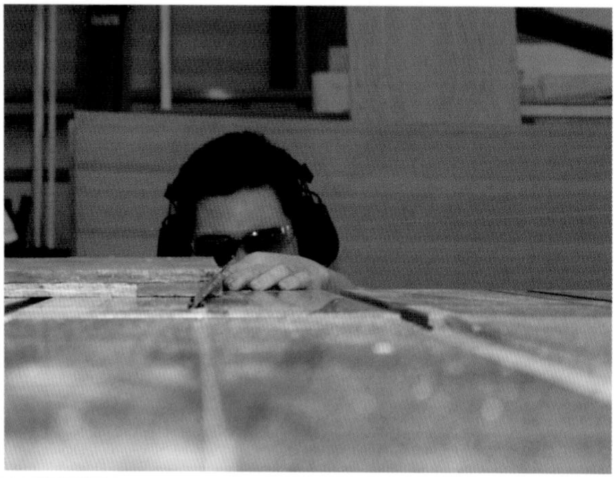

2

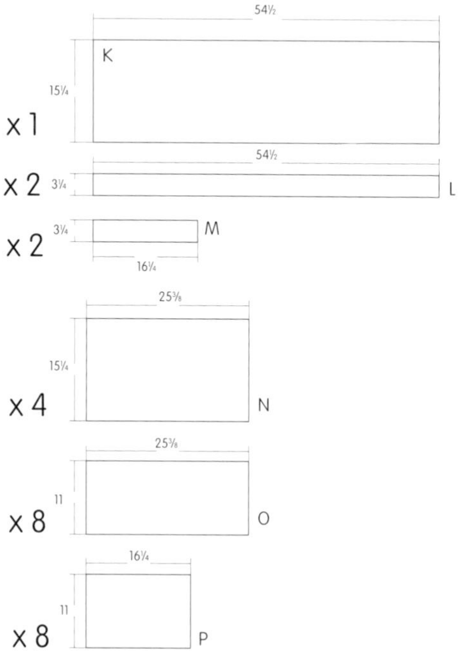
54½
K
15¼
x 1
54½
x 2
3¼
L
3¼
M
x 2
16¼
25⅜
15¼
x 4
N
25⅜
11
x 8
O
16¼
11
x 8
P

Cut the ½in OSB to the following sizes:
_One x 54½ x 15¼in (part K)
_Two x 54½ x 3¼in (part L)
_Two x 16¼ x 3¼in (part M)
_Four x 25⅜ x 15¼in (part N)
_Eight x 25⅜ x 11in (part O)
_Eight x 414 x 11in (part P)

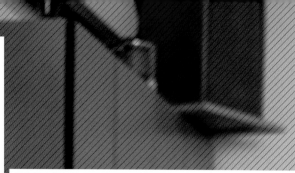

3

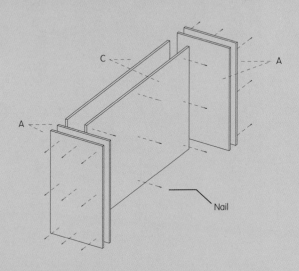

Assembling the sides and back
_Attach two part Cs together using finish nails, creating the back (part CC), applying wood glue between the surfaces.
_Attach two part As together using finish nails, creating one side (part AA), applying wood glue between the surfaces.
_Repeat with the other two part As to create the other side (part AA).

4

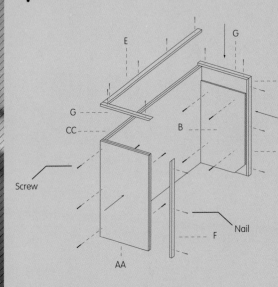

Completing the sides and back
_Attach each side (part AA) to the back (part CC) as shown, using the 2½in screws.
_Cap the top of part CC with part E, the tops of parts AA with parts G, and the fronts of AA with parts F using finish nails and matching the miters as shown (apply a coat of wood glue to both facing surfaces and miters to secure them).
_Attach part B to part AA using 1¾in screws, ensuring it is flush against the back (part CC) and that the diagonal corner is on the bottom facing as shown.
_Repeat with part B on the opposite side.

5

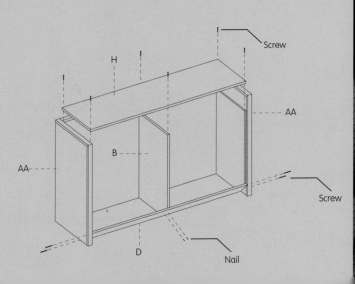

6

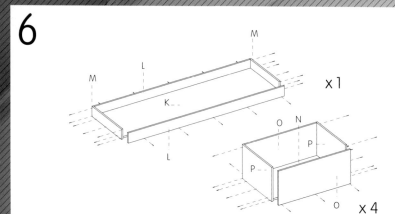

x1

x4

Assembling the drawers

_Set part K on a flat surface and create a box using two parts L
and two parts M (parts L should fit between parts M).
_After confirming positions, apply glue to the edges that touch
and nail them together using finish nails. This is your top drawer.
_Set part N on a flat surface and create a box, using two parts O
and two parts P (parts O should fit between parts P).
_After confirming positions, apply glue to the edges that touch
and nail them together using finish nails. This makes one bottom drawer.
_Repeat using parts N, O, and P to make a total of four bottom drawers.

7

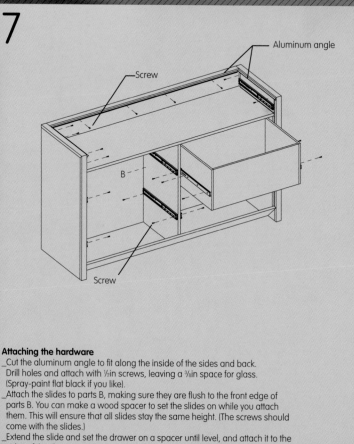

Aluminum angle

Screw

B

Screw

Attaching the hardware

_Cut the aluminum angle to fit along the inside of the sides and back.
Drill holes and attach with ½in screws, leaving a ⅜in space for glass.
(Spray-paint flat black if you like).
_Attach the slides to parts B, making sure they are flush to the front edge of
parts B. You can make a wood spacer to set the slides on while you attach
them. This will ensure that all slides stay the same height. (The screws should
come with the slides.)
_Extend the slide and set the drawer on a spacer until level, and attach it to the
sides of the drawer.
_Repeat for all drawers.

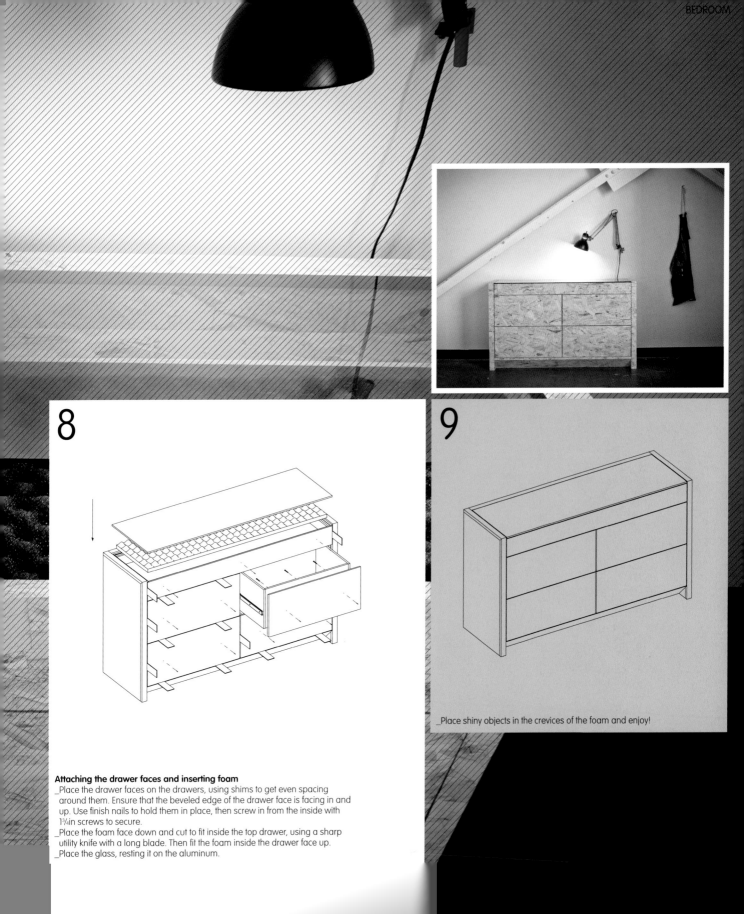

8

9

_Place shiny objects in the crevices of the foam and enjoy!

Attaching the drawer faces and inserting foam
_Place the drawer faces on the drawers, using shims to get even spacing around them. Ensure that the beveled edge of the drawer face is facing in and up. Use finish nails to hold them in place, then screw in from the inside with 1¾in screws to secure.
_Place the foam face down and cut to fit inside the top drawer, using a sharp utility knife with a long blade. Then fit the foam inside the drawer face up.
_Place the glass, resting it on the aluminum.

RETREAT

MAARTJE DROS AND FRANÇOIS LOMBARTS

In answer to a brief for sleeping places for guests at an exhibition and symposium in Zurich, designers Maartje Dros and François Lombarts experimented with a series of different sleeping arrangements to find what effect these might have on the common space and the dynamics of the participants. The solutions ranged from the most basic sleeping places through to self-contained modules. One of the latter is shown here.

It was an exercise in finding intimacy within the existing architecture, but also in creating it. The different sleeping proposals look for the line between private and public, sealing themselves off from their surroundings yet at the same time being exposed. The most basic sleeping units could be considered somewhat confrontational in their simplicity and positioning, and form a contrast to the more isolated modules.

The sleeping module shown here is built from wooden pallets. Wooden frames are attached to the pallets and sealed off with scaffolding cloth, creating a more intimate space. The step-by-step instructions overleaf can be adapted according to the surroundings and desires of the maker.

Retreats was a solution for sleeping modules for the Faculty of Invisibility's "Assembly" symposium. The series of different sleeping situations were spread out within the exhibition space of Shedhalle in Zurich, Switzerland, 2010.

You will need:

Materials

_Two twin-size mattresses

_Four pallets approx. 40 x 40in (part A)

_Two wooden beams (2¾ x 2¾ x 100in)

_Fifteen wooden boards (¾ x 4¾ x 95in)

_Two wooden boards (¾ x 4¾ x 118in)

_Twelve wooden boards (¾ x 3 x 40in)

_Large box of screws, 1¾in long

_Fifty screws, 2in long

_Scaffolding cloth (158 x 355in)

_Rope

_Four metal washers

Tools

_Drill

_Drill bit for predrilling

_Saw

_Staple gun and staples

1

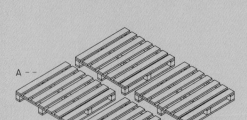

Pallet sizes vary from country to country. It is important that you choose and adjust the size of your pallets according to the measurements of your mattress. For this design, we used two twin-size mattresses and four 40 x 40in pallets. Use the following dimensions as a guide and adjust based on your mattress size and needs.

Pallets
Pallets form the base of the design.
_Collect 4 similar pallets and arrange as shown (parts A).

2

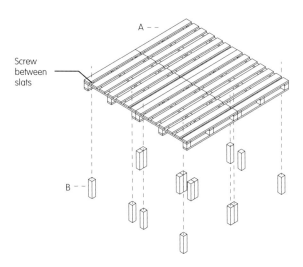

Screw between slats

Feet
Cut the 2¾ x 2¾in wood beams to the following length:
Sixteen x beams, 11in long (part B)
_Attach the feet as shown, placing each against the top cross support of the pallet.
_Predrill and screw them into place using the longer screws.

3

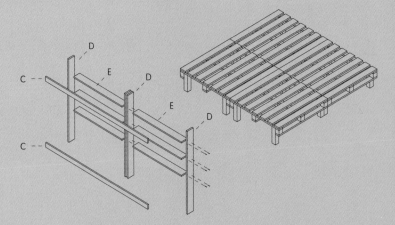

Headboard
Cut the ¾ x 4¾ x 95in boards into the following lengths:
_Two x 82in long (part C)
_Four x 55in long (part D)
_Six x 38¾in long (part E)

_Screw vertical planks (parts D) to the pallet.
_Screw shelves (parts E) in between.
_Connect vertical planks at top and bottom with side rails (parts C).

4

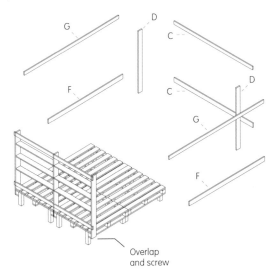

G

D

C

F

C

D

G

F

Overlap
and screw

Frame

Cut the ¾ x 4¾ x 95in boards into the following lengths:
_Two x 82in long (part C)
_Two x 55in long (part D)
_Two x 78¾in long (part F)
Cut the ¾ x 4¾ x 118in boards into the following lengths:
_Two x 99in long (part G)

_Screw vertical planks at the foot of the bed.
_Connect vertical planks to the upper parts and as side rails
  around the pallets.

5

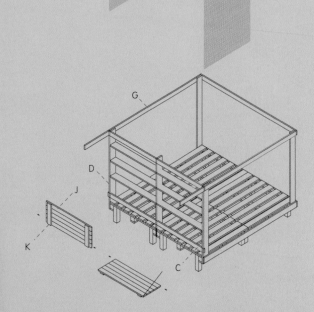

H

I

G

D

J

K

C

Canopy

For the canopy use scaffolding cloth or any semitransparent cloth for an open
yet intimate effect. For the configuration shown above, cut to the following
dimensions, adding a ¾in margin to each side for folding over:
_154x 82⅛in (part H)
_190⅜ x 39⅜in (part I)
_Fold the edge of the cloth and staple to the bottom side of the under frame.
_Stretch the cloth around the upper frame.
_Straighten the edges of the cloth by folding. Staple to the frame end.

Workstation

Cut the ¾ x 3 x 40in boards to the following lengths:
_Ten x 38⅜in long (part J)
_Four x 14¾in long (part K)

_Attach five parts J and two parts K to form one work surface. Repeat for an
  additional one.
_Use the horizontal beam (part C) on the front side as a support, while
  inserting two screws on either sides through the frame (part D) and into the
  end parts of the table. (Don't forget to add a metal washer before screwing
  the table to the frame in order to facilitate folding).
_Drill holes and attach rope to both table and frame. Hang the workstation.

6

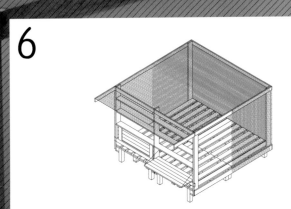

The variations are endless and personal.
_Add your mattress and enjoy your retreat!

A.O.CMS GLASS CABINET

CHRISTIAN HALLERÖD

The A.O.CMS display cabinet was created for the Stockholm store of the fashion brand of the same name. The brand, A.O.CMS, makes premium wardrobe staple pieces that are a testament to simplicity and endurance.

Echoing that simplicity, two sister cabinets were designed to carry a large number of products in a small area of a few square feet. One has display shelves that are removable, which allows for flexibility in the display—for instance, a single shelf can easily be placed on the cash desk—and the other highlights a single article, which proudly hangs behind glass as though it were an exhibit in a museum.

You will need:

Materials

_Four 1¼ x 1¼ in hardwood boards, at least 71in long

_Six ½ x 1¾in hardwood boards, at least 32in long

_One ½ x 28 x 16in hardwood board

_Two pieces clear tempered glass ¼ x 26½ x 54⅜in (have your local glass store cut and temper them for you)

_Wood glue

_Wood finish

_Screws

_Small finish nails

_Metal clothes rail and end brackets

_Hanger

Tools

_Table saw

_Router

_¼ in straight bit for router

_Drill

_Countersink bit

_Punch for small nails

_Hammer

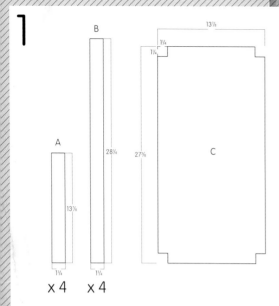

1

Cut the ½ x 1¾in boards to the following lengths:
_Four x 13⅞in long (part A)
_Four x 28¼in long (part B)
_Cut the ½ x 28 x 16in board as shown to make part C,
 notching all four corners 1¼in each direction.

2

Detail
part D

Detail
part E

_Cut the 1¼ x 1¼in boards to the following lengths:
 Four x 69¾in long.
_Use the router to cut a groove in each board.
_When looking down the board, make two with the
 groove ⅜in from the right side (part D) and two
 with the groove ⅜in from the left side (part E).

3

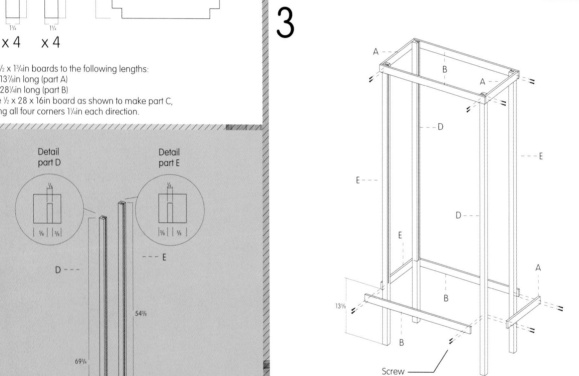

_Predrill with the countersink bit and assemble as shown,
 using screws and wood glue where the boards overlap.
_The top boards should be flush with the top of parts D
 and E.
_The lower boards are 13⅝in from the ground to the
 bottom edge.

5

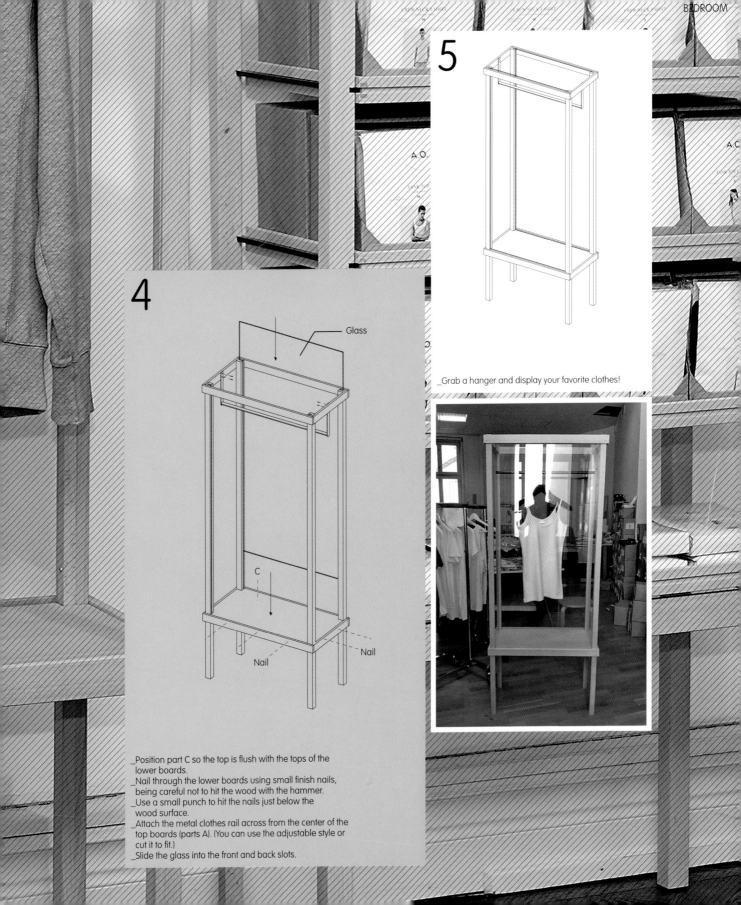

_Grab a hanger and display your favorite clothes!

4

Glass

C

Nail

Nail

_Position part C so the top is flush with the tops of the lower boards.
_Nail through the lower boards using small finish nails, being careful not to hit the wood with the hammer.
_Use a small punch to hit the nails just below the wood surface.
_Attach the metal clothes rail across from the center of the top boards (parts A). (You can use the adjustable style or cut it to fit.)
_Slide the glass into the front and back slots.

QUILT

CHRIS RUCKER OF RUCKERCORP

Rucker has always been surrounded by quilting. His mother is an avid quilter, as was her mother before her. Although Rucker himself liked them, and liked the rituals connected with them—making quilts for the birth of a child, a marriage, and so on—quilting in its traditional form was not on his agenda.

When he began making his own "quilts," he made them out of the old moving blankets that he had used for years on construction sites to protect surfaces from damage, or to wrap cabinets that were in transit to job sites. Although they were worn, he didn't want to just throw them out, so the idea of turning them into quilts, and ultimately transforming them into precious or sacred objects that carried all the marks and stains of their years of use, appealed to him.

You will need:

Materials

_Moving blanket (only one is needed to create the alternating thread pattern; add more as needed to vary the colors)

_Scrap fabric 60 x 70in

Tools

_Sharp scissors

_Sewing machine with large needle

_Seam ripper

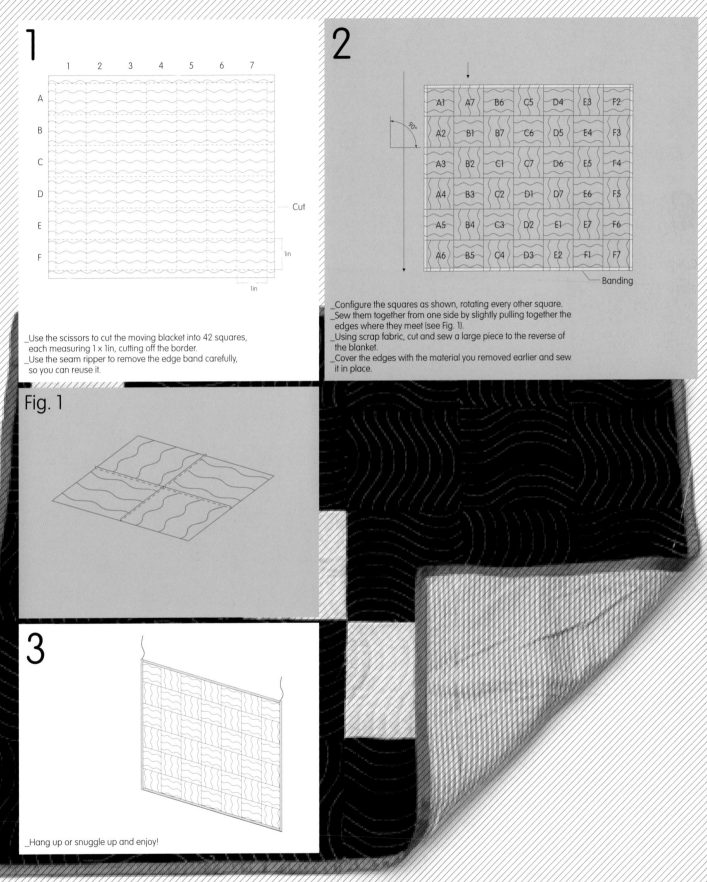

1

	1	2	3	4	5	6	7
A							
B							
C							
D							
E							
F							

Cut

1in

1in

_Use the scissors to cut the moving blacket into 42 squares,
each measuring 1 x 1in, cutting off the border.
_Use the seam ripper to remove the edge band carefully,
so you can reuse it.

2

90°

A1	A7	B6	C5	D4	E3	F2
A2	B1	B7	C6	D5	E4	F3
A3	B2	C1	C7	D6	E5	F4
A4	B3	C2	D1	D7	E6	F5
A5	B4	C3	D2	E1	E7	F6
A6	B5	C4	D3	E2	F1	F7

Banding

_Configure the squares as shown, rotating every other square.
_Sew them together from one side by slightly pulling together the
edges where they meet (see Fig. 1).
_Using scrap fabric, cut and sew a large piece to the reverse of
the blanket.
_Cover the edges with the material you removed earlier and sew
it in place.

Fig. 1

3

_Hang up or snuggle up and enjoy!

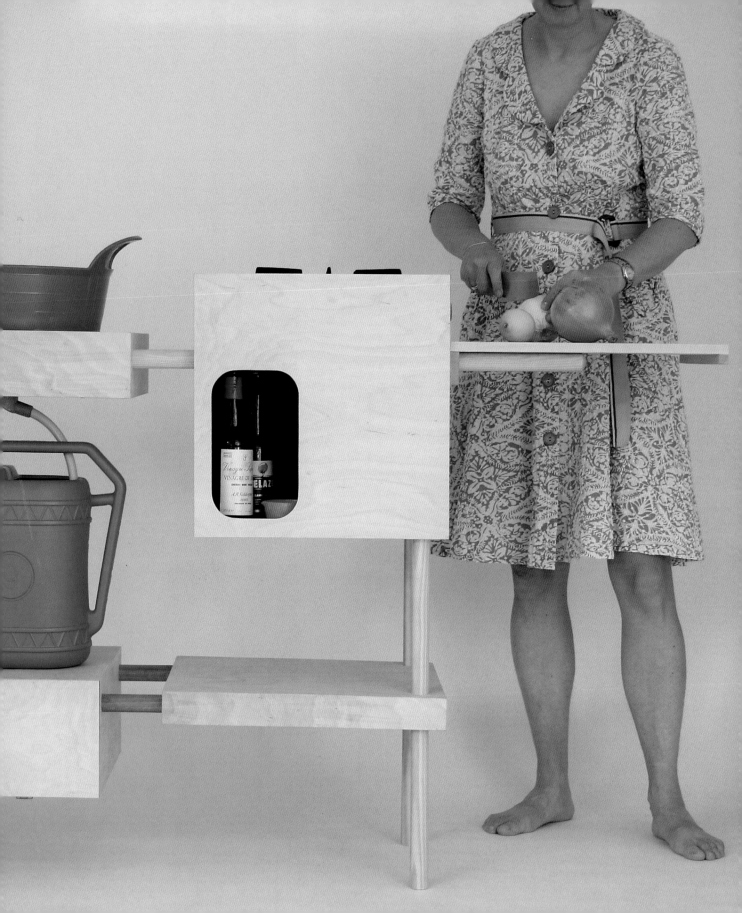

6.
OUTDOOR

Throw out that plastic lawn set (or turn them into some Sea Chairs) and get with these outdoor designs. They look so good, you might just want to pitch a tent. The convenience of Outdoor Kitchen by Studiomama will have you spoiled and looking like one smart host at your next cookout. Wash up at the sink and serve up an intimate dinner for two on Chimney Pot Stools, a clever way of using clay chimney stacks to make perfect stools and a table. Oh! And don't forget the candles. We cover those in the Miscellaneous chapter. If things heat up and you find yourself needing a little privacy, get cosy behind Odla, an easy-to-make screen created from off-the-shelf perforated metal. Put what you've learned in this book to the test and design yourself a planter box. Grapevines would look and taste great at your next cookout.

ODLA

DANIEL FRANZÉN, ADAM ALMQUIST, AND OSCAR TITELMAN

The Odla series of products for the garden is produced by a Swedish company focusing on the rehabilitation of ex-cons into "normal" society. The brief for this design was for a construction that almost anybody could build.

The series was designed by Franzén, together with Adam Almquist and Oscar Titelman.

You will need:

Materials

_Five pine boards, 1¾ x 2¾ x 67in

_Powder-coated perforated metal, at least 45 x 61in

_Screws, 2¾in and 3⅞in long

_Wooden plugs that fit the screw hole size (optional). You can also make these using a plug cutter and the scrap wood.

_Plastic or rubber feet, approx. 1¾ x 1¾in

_Wood glue

Tools

_Saw

_Router with a ⅜in straight bit

_Drill

_Countersink bit

_Metal shears

1

x2 x1 x1 x2

45

19⅝ D

47¼ B

44 C

66 A

61

E

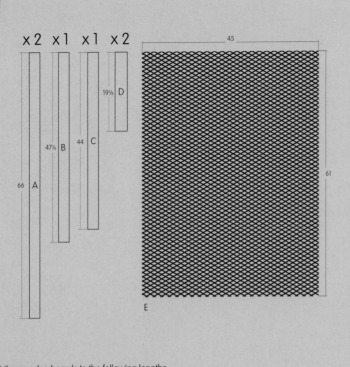

Cut the wooden boards to the following lengths:
_Two x 66in (part A)
_One x 47¼in (part B)
_One x 44in (part C)
_Two x 19⅝in (part D)
_Use the metal shears to cut the perforated metal to 45 x 61in.

2

A

5¾ 1

B

1

C

⅜
⅜

Detail

x2 x1 x1

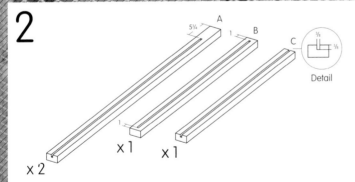

Use the router to cut the following ⅜in-wide x ⅝in-deep grooves:
_Two x part A from one end, stopping 5¾in from the opposite end
_One x part B from end to end, leaving 1in on each end.
_One x part C for the entire length.

3

B

Screw

A

A

D

C

D

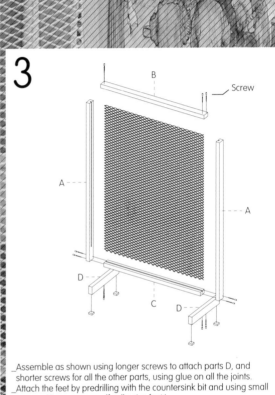

_Assemble as shown using longer screws to attach parts D, and shorter screws for all the other parts, using glue on all the joints.
_Attach the feet by predrilling with the countersink bit and using small screws. (Or use some self-adhesive feet.)

4

_Let some plants grow and enjoy your privacy!

CHIMNEY POT SERIES

JONATHAN LEGGE

Like lots of good ideas, this series evolved from a spontaneous action. A need for an extra table, a neighbor's chimney pot, and a sheet of wood. It worked for the evening in question, and the next day Jonathan decided to refine the idea into a more stable piece of furniture.

There is no big concept, no attempt at something particularly new, just a simple table fabricated from an off-the-shelf chimney pot and wood. They are not objects asking for any great intellectual understanding—it is really just a simple idea, but the result is a series of objects defined and created by their use.

You will need:

Materials

_Two wooden boards, 29½ x 29½ x 1¾in (cedar and white oak are both good woods for outdoor use)

_Wood screws, 3⅛in long

_Wood glue

_Wood sealant for outdoor use

_Two clay roll-top chimney pots, 17¾in tall

_One clay roll-top chimney pot, 29½in tall

Tools

_Jigsaw

_Sandpaper

_Drill

_Drill bit, 3⅞in diameter

1

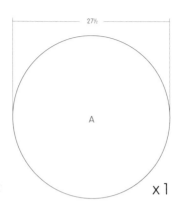

27½

A

x 1

12¼

B

x 2

7⅝*

C

x 3

Cut the wood into circles of the
following diameters:
_One x 27½in (part A)
_Two x 12¼in (part B)
_Three x 7⅝in (part C)
* this dimension should be slightly smaller
  than the inside lip of the clay pot as it needs
  to rest inside.
_Use coarse sandpaper to refine the shape.

2

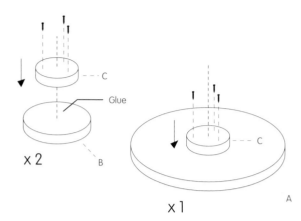

C

Glue

x 2

B

C

x 1

A

_Attach one part B and one part C as shown, using
 wood glue where they meet. Secure with screws, but
 keep the screws away from the central area because
 this will be drilled in the next step.
_Repeat this so that you have two small disk sets. These
 will be the tops for your stools.
_Attach one part A and one part C as shown, using
 wood glue where they meet and securing with screws.
 This will be your tabletop.

3

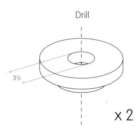

Drill

3⅞

x 2

_Drill a 3⅞in hole through the connected stool tops.
 This is optional, but allows water to drain so that it
 will stay reasonably dry. The size of the bit is really
 up to you.

4

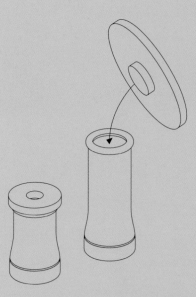

_Flip the tops over and set on the chimney pots.
_The taller pot is for the table.
_Sand the tops and sides to a smooth finish.
_Seal the wood with a coat of clear sealant suitable for
the outdoors.

5

_Pull up a chimney stool and enjoy!

OUTDOOR KITCHEN

NINA TOLSTRUP AND JACK MAMA OF STUDIOMAMA

When the weather is up to it, this construction will let you do all your chopping, peeling, and cooking outside. The outdoor kitchen comprises a gas cooking hob, a bucket sink, a chopping board, and storage for crockery, utensils, and a few food ingredients. Water is connected from the garden hose and waste water is collected in a watering can placed beneath the sink, so that it can be reused.

Although the product instructions give different options for construction, depending on level of skill and access to tools, you'll need to be confident in the workshop to embark on this project. Alternatively, you could get a skilled carpenter to make it for you.

All the components can be sourced from hardware stores. The boxes are constructed from ply and the structure from broomsticks and some screws. The surface treatment can be tailored to suit personal preference—the version shown here was treated with Osmo oil.

You will need:

Materials

_Two ¼in plywood, 96 x 48in

_One ½in plywood, 48 x 48in

_¾ x ¾in batten, 16½ft long

_⅝in timber

_Two castors, 5in (metal rim heavy duty)

_Broom handles, 1⅛in diameter, 28ft long

_Gate valve (compression fitting), ⅝ x ⅝in

_Copper pipe, ⅞in diameter, 3ft long

_Solder ring/fitting reducer, ⅞ to ⅝in

_One ⅝in diameter copper pipe, 6in long

_Two pipe clips

_One ⅞ to ⅝in copper pipe reducer

_One M6 x 25 washer

_One M6 x 20 washer

_M4 screws, 1in

_M6 screws, 2⅛in

_Cross dowels M6

_Cross dowel bolts M6 x 3⅛in

_Hinges

_Hose connector

_Plastic bucket

_Watering can

_Foker cast iron single gas burner

_Gas flask

_Osmo finishing oil

_Angled sink waste, 1¼in

Tools

_Bench saw

_Router

_Drill and ⅝in drill bit

_Countersink drill bit

_1⅛in Forstner drill bit

_Pinkgrip D4 wood glue

_Sandpaper

_Adhesive tape

_Clamps

_Vise

_Tape measure

_Pencil for marking up

_Center punch

_Chalk

_Micrometer

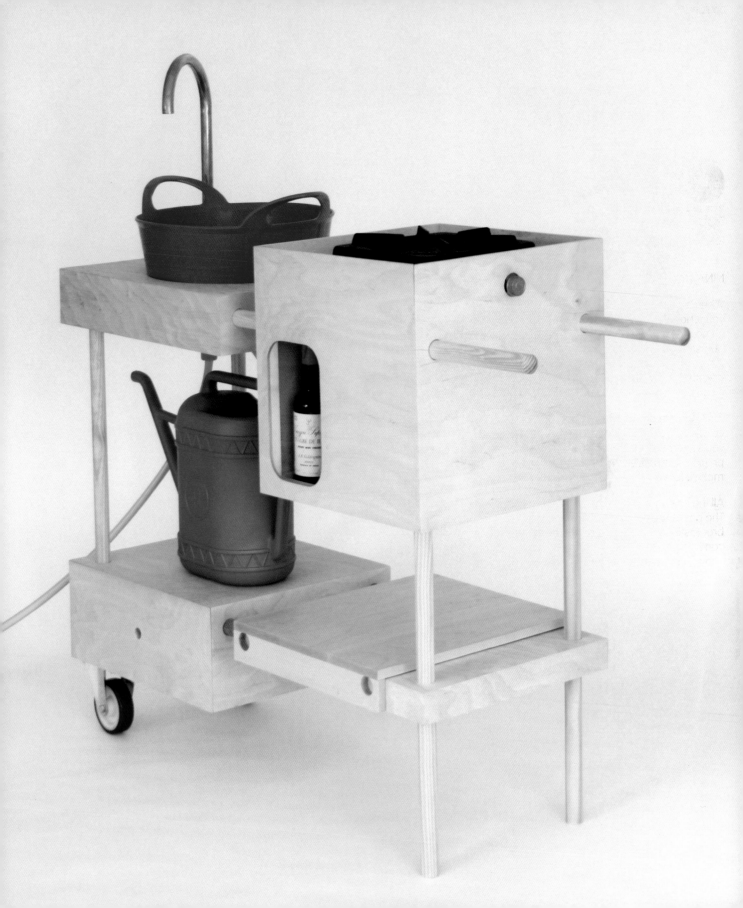

1

Miter edges highlighted in gray

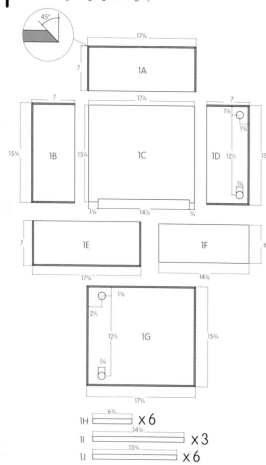

45°

1A — 17¾ × 7

1B — 7 × 15¾

1C — 17¼ × 15¼

1D — 7 × 15¾, 1⅛, 1⅛, 12½, 1⅛, ¾

1E — 7 × 17¼

1F — 14⅞ × 6

1G — 17¼ × 15¼, 1⅛, 2½, 12½, 1⅛

1H — 6⅜ × 6

1I — 14⅞ × 3

1J — 13¾ × 6

Drawer box

Cut the ¼in plywood to the following sizes:
_One x 17¾ x 7in (part 1A)
_One x 7 x 15¾in (part 1B)
_One x 7 x 15¾in (part 1D)
_One x 17¾ x 7in (part 1E)
_One x 17¾ x 15¾in (part 1G)
Cut the ½in plywood to the following sizes:
_One x 17¼ x 15¼in (part 1C)
_One x 14⅞ x 6in (part 1F)
Cut the ¾ x ¾in batten to the following lengths:
_Six x 6⅜in (part 1H)
_Three x 14⅞in (part 1I)
_Six x 13¾in (part 1J)
_Use a bench saw or router to miter the edges marked in gray above.
_Locate and drill all the cutouts/holes as shown above.

2

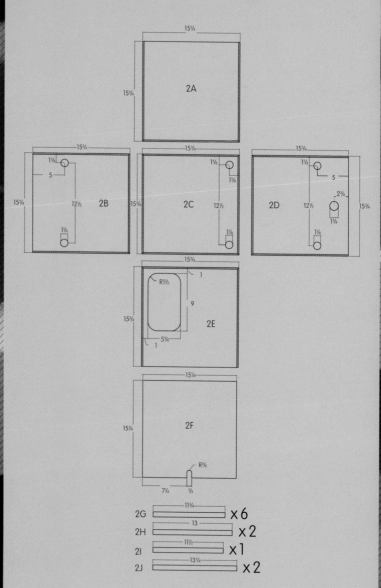

2A — 15¼ × 15¾

2B — 15¾ × 15¾, 1⅛, 5, 12½, 1⅛

2C — 15¾ × 15¾, 1⅛, 1⅛, 12½, 1⅛

2D — 15¾ × 15¾, 1⅛, 5, 12½, 2⅜, 1⅜, 1⅛

2E — 15¾ × 15¾, R1½, 1, 9, 5⅜, 1

2F — 15¼ × 15¼, R⅜, 7¼, ¾

2G — 11¾ × 6

2H — 13 × 2

2I — 11½ × 1

2J — 13¾ × 2

Burner box

Cut the ¼in plywood to the following sizes:
_Five x 15¾ x 15¾in (parts 2A, 2B, 2C, 2D, 2E)
_One x 15¼ x 15¼in (part 2F)
Cut the ¾ x ¾in batten to the following lengths:
_Six x 11¾in (part 2G)
_Two x 13in (part 2H)
_One x 11½in (part 2I)
_Two x 13¾in (part 2J)
_Use a bench saw or router to miter the edges marked in gray above.
_Locate and drill all the cutouts/holes as shown above.

4

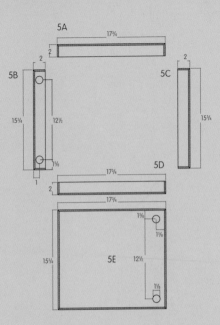

Chopping board box

Cut the ¼in plywood to the following sizes:
_One x 17¾ x 2in (part 5A)
_One x 2 x 15¾in (part 5B)
_One x 2 x 15¾in (part 5C)
_One x 17¾ x 2in (part 5D)
_One x 17¾ x 15¾in (part 5E)
_Use a bench saw or router to miter the edges marked in gray above.
_Locate and drill all the cutouts/holes as shown above.

3

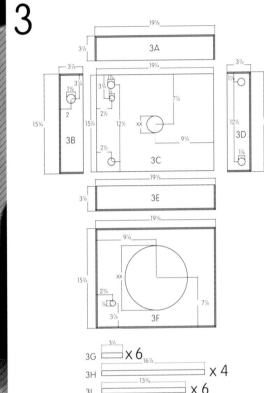

Sink box

Cut the ¼in plywood to the following sizes:
_One x 19⅝ x 3⅞in (part 3A)
_One x 3⅞ x 15¾in (part 3B)
_One x 3⅞ x 15¾in (part 3D)
_One x 19⅝ x 3⅞in (part 3E)
_One x 19⅝ x 15¾in (part 3F). Note for hole xx: this diameter could vary, depending on the sink bowl used.
Cut the ½in plywood to the following size:
_One x 19¼ x 15¼in (part 3C). Note for hole xx: this diameter could vary, depending on the sink bowl used.
Cut the ¾ x ¾in batten to the following lengths:
_Six x 3½in (part 3G)
_Four x 16⅞in (part 3H)
_Six x 13¾in (part 3I)
_Use a bench saw or router to miter the edges marked in gray above.
_Locate and drill all the cutouts/holes as shown above.

5

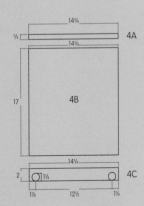

Chopping board

Cut the ⅝in wood to the following sizes:
_One x 14¾ x ¾in (part 4A)
_One x 14¾ x 17in (part 4B)
_One x 14¾ x 2in (part 4C)
_Locate and drill both the cutouts/holes as shown above.

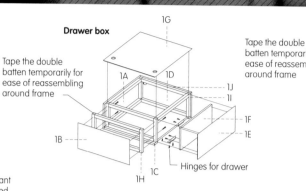

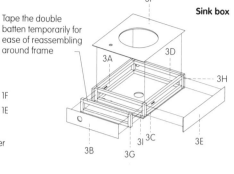

Drawer box

Tape the double batten temporarily for ease of reassembling around frame

1G
1A · 1D · 1J · 1I · 1F · 1E · 1B · 1C · 1H

Hinges for drawer

Sink box

Tape the double batten temporarily for ease of reassembling around frame

3F · 3A · 3D · 3H · 3B · 3G · 3I · 3C · 3E

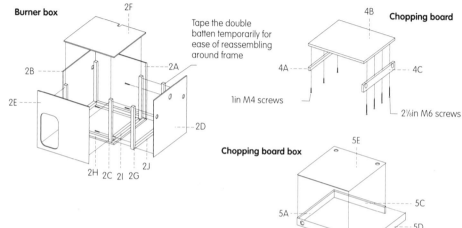

Burner box

2F · 2B · 2A · 2E · 2D · 2H · 2C · 2I · 2G · 2J

Tape the double batten temporarily for ease of reassembling around frame

Chopping board

4B · 4A · 4C

1in M4 screws

2¹⁄₈in M6 screws

Chopping board box

5E · 5A · 5C · 5D · 5B

Assembly

_Construct the boxes while not attached to the frame, as shown. This allows for a neat final construction.

_Since the boxes are first made up, then disassembled before attaching to the frame, it is important that some of the joints are not glued. Assemble the box faces as shown, and glue and clamp them together as required until each assembly is dry.

_For the drawer box, be sure to glue/clamp the inner and outer board (parts 1E and 1F) prior to attaching the two hinges. Note: You will not attach the drawer face (parts 1E and 1F) to the remaining drawer box assembly until after the frame is completely assembled.

_Fit the double battens (remembering to temporarily tape them) into the box assemblies. Fit the remaining batten structures into the boxes as shown, using glue as required. For double battens, drill holes in the battens, which will later accept screws. Use screws to assemble the chopping board as shown.

_Attach part 5C after the frame is completely assembled.

_Apply finishing oil/paint to the box assemblies as required.

Connection detail

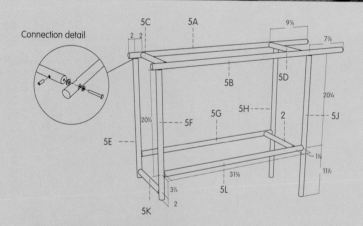

5C · 5A · 2 2 · 9⁷⁄₈ · 7⁷⁄₈ · 5B · 5D · 20¼ · 5H · 5G · 2 · 5J · 20¼ · 5F · 5E · 1¼ · 11½ · 3¼ · 31⅜ · 5L · 5K · 2

Frame preparation

Note: The illustration here is to be used for initial identification/measurements. Once the broom handles are cut to length, the frame connections (explained below) will need to be coordinated with the box installations explained in Step 8.

Cut the 1⅛in-diameter broom handles to the following lengths:
_Four x 11¾in (parts 5C, 5D, 5K, 5I)
_Two x 47in (parts 5A, 5B)
_Two x 25½in (parts 5E, 5F)
_Two x 31¾in (parts 5H, 5J)
_Two x 34¾in (parts 5G, 5L)
_Mark up all the connection locations on the cut broom handles as shown.
_Tape the two broomsticks together (see Fig. 1) to prevent them from twisting during drilling. Drill all large recesses (1⅛in diameter) ⅓in deep and small recesses (⅝in diameter) ½in deep on the opposite side (see Fig. 2).
_Use a valley-shaped rest (see Fig. 3) to hold the broom handles in place as you drill the holes for the cross dowels.
_Clamp the broom handles (see Fig. 4) vertically in a table vise and drill the holes along the length of the broom handle for insertion of the cross dowel bolt. Start each hole with a center punch to reduce the chances of going off-course.

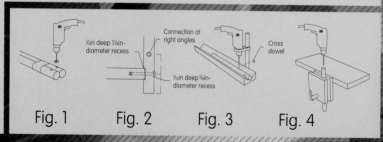

⅓in deep 1⅛in-diameter recess

Connection at right angles

Cross dowel

½in deep ⅝in-diameter recess

Fig. 1   Fig. 2   Fig. 3   Fig. 4

8

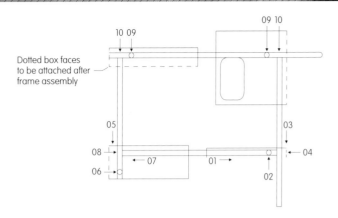

Dotted box faces
to be attached after
frame assembly

Frame assembly

1_Slide the broom construction into the chopping board box.
2_Connect the cross broom 5I to 5H and 5J.
3_Slide brooms 5H and 5J into chopping board box.
4_Connect the vertical brooms 5H and 5J to 5G and 5L.
5_Slide brooms 5E and 5F into the drawer box.
6_Connect cross broom 5K (see Figs 5, 6, 7).
6a_Slide broom 5E into the drawer box (Fig. 5).
6b_Rotate so the connection 5E–5K faces outward (Fig. 5).
6c_Position broom 5K (Fig. 6).
6d_Connect brooms 5E and 5F to 5K (Fig. 6).
6e_Rotate through 90 degrees (Fig. 6).
6f_Slide broom 5G into the drawer box (Fig. 7).
6g_Connect brooms 5E and 5G (Fig. 7). Repeat with brooms 5F and 5L.
7_Slide frame construction into the drawer box.
8_Connect 5E–5G and 5F–5L.
9_Slide brooms 5A and 5B through the burner and sink boxes.
10_Shift the boxes along the brooms to access connections.
_Using double battens, attach the remaining faces of the boxes with
 screws through the predrilled double battens. Attach the drawer face via
 the two hinges on the drawer box.
_Place the chopping board on top of the chopping board box.

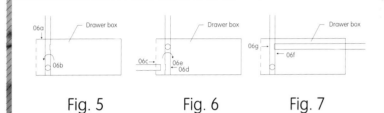

Fig. 5   Fig. 6   Fig. 7

9

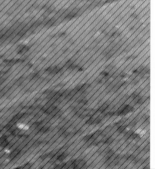

8

14⅛

⁷⁄₈in-diameter pipe

Reducing coupler

Pipe clip

Gate valve

Garden hose attachment

⅝in-dia. pipe

Pipe tap

_Use a pipe bender (see Fig. 8) to carefully bend
 the copper pipe to the radius shown above. Be careful
 not to crimp the pipe while you are bending it.
_Use two pipe clips to fix the plumbing to the battens with
 screws (see Fig. 9).

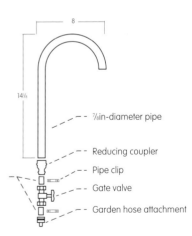

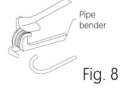

Pipe
bender

Fig. 8

Fig. 9

10

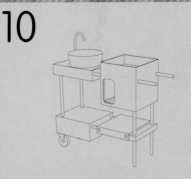

_Attach the heavy-duty castors and insert the
 sink basin and gas burner.
_Cook a delicious meal with your outdoor
 kitchen and enjoy!

7.
MISC.

Small, but mighty! Here's a collection of accessories that pack a designer punch. And if you've been looking to get your hands dirty, there are two rock solid projects to get you on your way. Portland—named after the cement used in the creation of these stunning candlesticks—are cast in PVC and broken (yes, broken) to various lengths to create the artistic base. Chen Chen and Kai Williams are no strangers to the hands-on approach to design. Scraps of granite and found objects get preserved in Rockite to form these modern-day fossils, perfectly shaped to bookend your DIY books. Duplicate the efforts of your hard work by hanging the simply shaped Circle Mirror from Jean-Philippe Bonzon's Geometric collection. Lower your brow and crank up the tunes to the worksite-inspired, high-tech meets low-tech Radiola Table, which goes to show that inspiration can come from unexpected places.

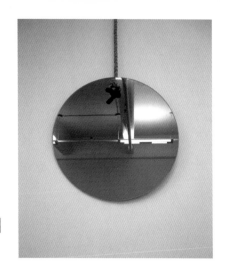

GEOMETRIC: CIRCLE MIRROR

JEAN-PHILIPPE BONZON

The pieces for Jean-Philippe Bonzon's Geometric series, of which Circle Mirror forms a part, were created as objects that are easy to manufacture and easy to make yourself.

This 24in-diameter mirror, which employs just a hole and a piece of rope, is very easy to assemble. You just need to go to your favorite glaziers and ask them to cut it to size for you—show them your construction drawing with the three dimensions detailed opposite. Then buy a nice piece of rope; the best is probably one made of natural fibers for that antique look, but ropes are available in many different beautiful colors at your local DIY store if you want to match it to your other furnishings.

Follow the instructions opposite and then enjoy looking at yourself in your new mirror. You can make a whole wall of mirrors, using different diameters, large or small. Hang them all in a row, or hang several from one piece of rope. With all those reflections, great effects are guaranteed!

You will need:

Materials

_Mirror, approx. 24in diameter

_Natural rope, 1¾in diameter, 6ft long

_Scrap piece of plywood, slightly larger than the mirror

Tools

_Knife

_Drill

_Diamond drill bit for glass, 2in diameter

_Clear packing tape

_Dust mask

_Water bottle with squirt-type top

_Glass cleaner

1

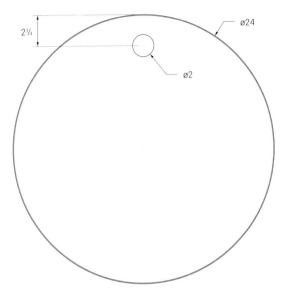

2¾

ø24

ø2

_Place the mirror face down on the scrap plywood (being careful not to scratch the surface).
_Mark the hole location as shown and place clear packing tape over the circle where it will be drilled.
_Using light pressure, slowly drill through the mirror (wear your dust mask so that you don't breathe in the glass particles).
_Keep the bit cool by squirting water on it, occasionally lifting the bit to allow water to get in.
_Flip the mirror over and clean up the hole from the other side by taping it as before and lightly drilling it again.
_Remove the tape and clean the mirror with glass cleaner.
_Another option is to take your mirror to your local glazier. Less risk of cutting yourself!

2

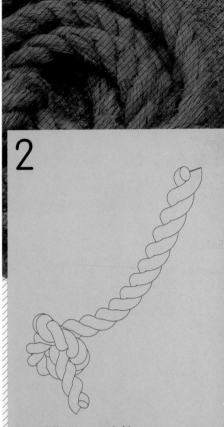

_Tie a solid knot in one end of the rope.
_Measure how long you would like the mirror to hang and use a knife to cut the rope to length.

3

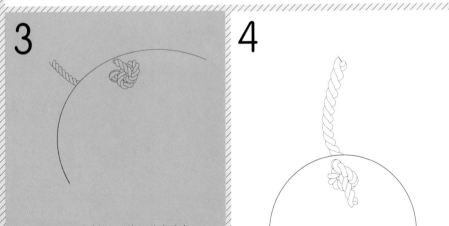

_Pass the other end of the rope through the hole.

4

_Attach the rope to a hook and check yourself out!

RADIOLA TABLE

STUDIOMK27

The "Prostheses and Grafts" project—a 16-piece collection—was conceived by the team of architects at StudioMK27. The highly functional furniture came from the project sites of the office, constructed anonymously by civil construction laborers in Brazil. All of the furniture in the exhibition was used at the sites.

These pieces then underwent small modifications at the hands of the designers and architects at StudioMK27 before a brief selection was gathered and presented at the Micasa Vol B store in São Paulo in March 2010.

Radiola Table, a bench table with an iPod dock, was numbered 01 in the exhibition. It works as a support for any type of small music device that can be plugged into the speaker stand.

You will need:

Materials

_Two ¾in thick wooden boards, 24 x 24in

_Screws

_Two speakers, approx. 3½in diameter, with audio jacks/connectors

_iPod/iPhone universal adapter

Tools

_Saw

_Drill

_Router

_Soldering gun

1

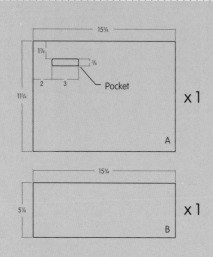

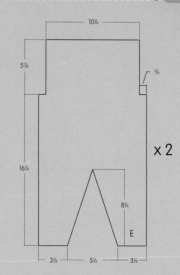

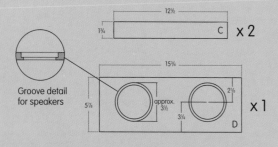

_Cut the ¾in-thick wooden boards according to the dimensions above.
The pocket slot in Part A is 15mm deep.
_With a router, create a pocket/slot in Part A as shown.
_In Part D, create a groove detail large enough to fit the two speakers.

2

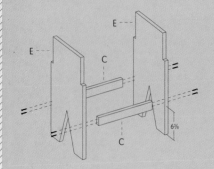

Legs
_Place the horizontal braces (parts C) between the sides of the stand (parts E) and attach them with screws. Make sure the bottom of the horizontal braces are 6⅜in from the base of the sides.

3

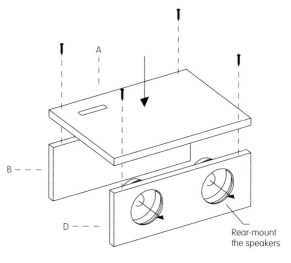

Speaker cabinet
_Rear-mount the two speakers into the pocket grooves on the back of the front face (part D). Mount the jacks/connectors and solder the wiring.
_Locate the iPod/iPhone universal adapter in the pocket on the top of the stand (part A). Drill a hole through the pocket in order to connect the adapter to the speakers.
_Mount the top of the stand (part A) to the front and back faces (parts B and D) with screws.
_Optionally, you can get a grille cover (e.g. from www.parts-express.com) and mount the cover prior to mounting the speakers.

4

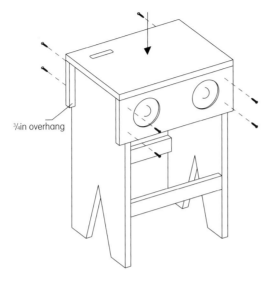

¾in overhang

_Mount the speaker cabinet on the legs with eight screws.
The speaker cabinet should extend out past the legs by
¾in on either side.

5

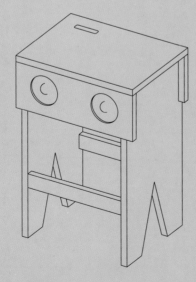

_Insert your iPod/iPhone, plug into the amplifier,
and rock out!

PORTLAND

DAVID TAYLOR

Portland makes a statement. Robust imagery and material selection give a brutal aspect to an object that is essentially used to create a warm and intimate ambiance.

The production of Portland is relatively simple and can be tackled by almost anybody with access to the most rudimentary tools. The beauty of this piece is that it's very easy to repeat but impossible to clone, making every piece individual. Each concrete part used is unique—the result of how it is made. As the concrete sticks are broken to length, a group of components of different lengths is gathered. Each piece has a different fracture pattern and a different set of imperfections from the casting, such as bubbles, sand marks, and cuts. It's from this group that pieces are brought together to form a candlestick.

David Taylor himself makes six or seven of these pieces at a time, which allows for a good margin of waste—sometimes a piece just doesn't work out and has to be binned, so he needs to make several in order to be happy with a few.

You will need:

Materials

_Copper sheet, ½in thick

_Hydraulic cement such as "Rockite"

_PVC electrical duct, 1¼in diameter, at least 55in long

_Copper pipe, 1¼in diameter, at least 2½in long

_Candleholder

_240 grit sandpaper

_Two M5 nuts, bolts, and washers

_Solder

Tools

_Hacksaw

_Bucket and paddle

_Tape

_Funnel (or a cut water bottle)

_Utility knife or Dremel

_Hot glue gun

_Metal shears

_Drill and ⅛in drill bit

_Soldering iron

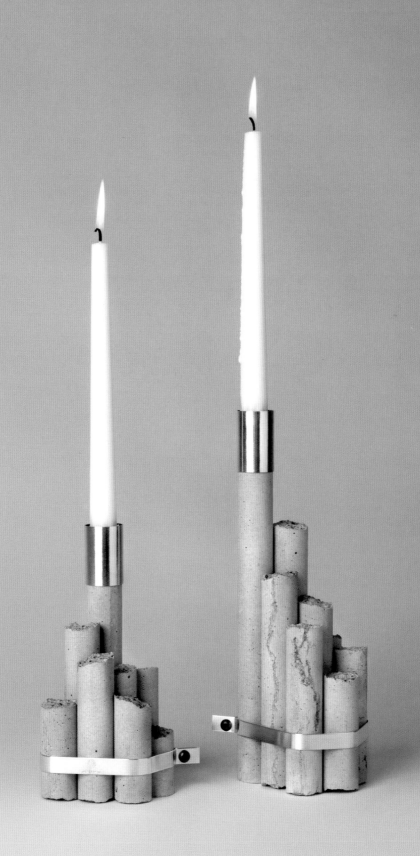

1

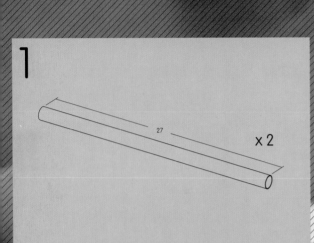

27

x 2

_Cut the PVC duct to two lengths of 27in each.

3

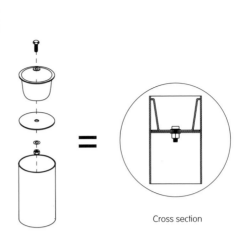

Cross section

_Cut a length of copper tube, about 2–2⅜in.
_Cut out a disk of copper from your sheet and solder it
 in place in the copper tube, making sure the top of the
 candleholder is flush with the top of the copper tube.
_Drill a ⅛in hole in the soldered disk and attach the
 candleholder with an M5 nut, bolt, and washer.

2

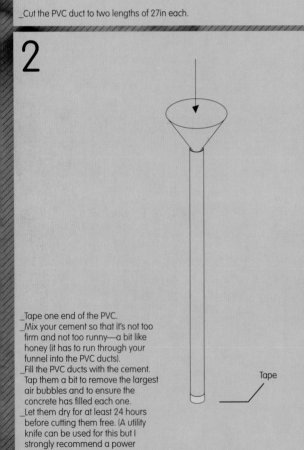

Tape

_Tape one end of the PVC.
_Mix your cement so that it's not too
 firm and not too runny—a bit like
 honey (it has to run through your
 funnel into the PVC ducts).
_Fill the PVC ducts with the cement.
 Tap them a bit to remove the largest
 air bubbles and to ensure the
 concrete has filled each one.
_Let them dry for at least 24 hours
 before cutting them free. (A utility
 knife can be used for this but I
 strongly recommend a power
 tool like a Dremel.)
_Once removed from the duct, let the
 concrete sticks dry properly—for at
 least another 24 hours.

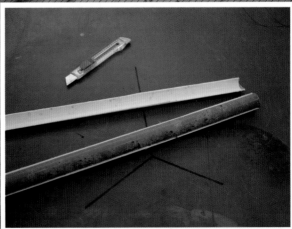

4

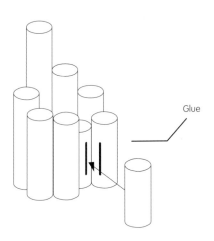

Glue

_Use your hands to break the concrete into eight different
lengths. Remember to make one much longer than the
others for the candleholder itself.
_Compose your group of eight sticks and use hot glue to
stick them together. Make sure that there are no obvious
remnants of glue showing.

5

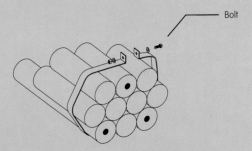

Bolt

_Use the metal shears to cut a copper band, ½in wide and long
enough to go all the way around the group of concrete sticks,
adding an extra 1½in.
_Finish the copper band and tube by sanding them with the 240
grit sandpaper.
_Wrap the copper band tightly around the body of the
candlestick, bending up the ends so they come neatly together.
_Drill a ⅛in hole through the end to allow an M5 nutbolt and
washer to be used to hold the sticks tightly together.
_Attach some feet by applying three generous blobs of glue to
the bottom of the candlestick.
_Allow the glue to set, then cut it back with a utility knife so that
the candlestick stands straight.

6

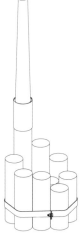

_Put the candleholder in place and insert a candle.
_Open your beer, light the candle, put on
some soft music, and let the love begin!

METAMORPHIC ROCK BOOKENDS

CHEN CHEN AND KAI WILLIAMS

Although visually very complex, at their core the Metamorphic Rock Bookends are also very basic. Their beauty comes from their simplicity.

Bookends need to be heavy and to have faces where they can mate with a book and a shelf. By putting a few scraps from a stone yard into a corner mold and filling it with cement, you can take useless yet beautiful industrial trash, and create an interesting composition with a functional purpose. The process stays the same for each Bookend but each composition is unique.

You will need:

Materials

_Rockite cement

_Plywood, ½ x 24 x 24in

_Aluminum flashing, 24 x 24in

_Plasticine

_Broken granite and marble

_Self-adhesive rubber feet

_Concrete sealant

_Scrap piece of 4–5in-diameter PVC pipe, approx. 3in long

_Water-based contact adhesive for laminate, such as Fastbond

_Screws, 1in long

Tools

_Drill bit slightly smaller than screws

_Two plastic cups

_Scale

_Stirring stick or scrap flooring tile

_Knife

_Wood file

_Foam brush

_Metal shears

_Saw

1

A

79

79

× 3

B

79

79

× 3

_Use the saw to cut the plywood into
three x 79 x 79in (part A).
_Use the metal shears to cut the flashing into
three x 79 x 79in (part B).

2

B

A

× 3

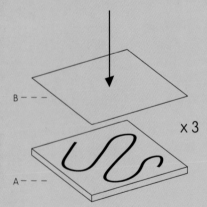

_Adhere the flashing (parts B) to the plywood (parts A)
using contact adhesive.
_Repeat so that you have three laminated squares.
_These may need to be clamped or weighted while the
glue is drying (follow adhesive instructions).

3

Screw

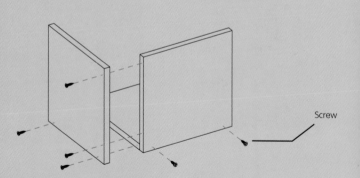

_Complete the mold by attaching the three squares with
screws, as shown. (Predrill the holes to get through the
aluminum flashing.)

4

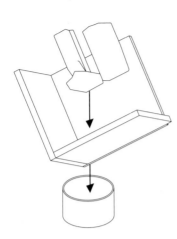

_Seal the mold by working a thin bead of plasticine into the corners.
_Hold the mold up by placing it on a section of PVC pipe (the mold does not necessarily have to be level).
_Place broken stones in the mold. Stones placed flush with the flashing will be visible in the final product.

5

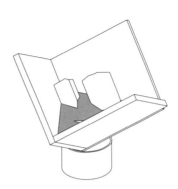

_Mix the cement: 1lb Rockite to 4oz water (always add cement to water and not the other way around). Mix well.
_Pour the cement into the mold.
_Wait at least 15 minutes before demolding.
_Remove the bookend from the mold. Unscrew the mold if the cement will not release.
_Clean up the faces, edges, and sharp corners with a file and knife.
_Wait at least one day before applying cement sealant.
_Place three self-adhesive rubber feet on your least favorite surface.

6

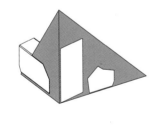
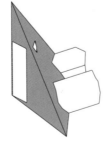

_Display prominently with your favorite books and enjoy!

Jean-Philippe Bonzon

Swiss-Argentinian Jean-Philippe Bonzon completed his studies in Switzerland, where he obtained a degree in Industrial Design and Products at ECAL, Lausanne, in July 2007. The designs he completed during his studies—including a boot removal device, a hair slide with bristles, and lamps made of cable binders—were praised for their choice and use of materials, as well as their ability to combine functional solutions with tongue-in-cheek humor. During the past few years, he has exhibited in New York (Vitra's store and ICFF), Cologne (IMM, Koelnmesse), Lausanne (MUDAC) and Milan (Furniture Fair), and he obtained third place at the Pavillon Suisse Le Corbusier contest in Paris. His project Modular Racks Staple obtained a Swiss Federal Design Award, which enabled him to exhibit in Zurich (Bellerive Museum). Jean-Philippe currently works in Shanghai.

www.jpbd.ch

Chen Chen and Kai Williams

Chen was born in Shanghai in 1985. His family later emigrated to Wyoming, moving to Canada before settling in New York City. While at Pratt, Chen spent a semester at the Gerrit Rietveld Academie in Amsterdam, where he was exposed to a nuanced and experimental design culture that has permanently influenced his practice. On graduation, he began working for Moss, rising to Display Director in 2010.

Williams was born in New York in 1984. During his studies at Pratt he worked doing high-end architectural metal fabrication and interned at 2x4, a graphic design company. After graduation he worked for the artist Tom Sachs as liaison between the artist and the studio, eventually overseeing installations at the Guggenheim in Bilbao and the preparations for his Lever House show.

Chen and Williams met while studying industrial design at Pratt Institute in Brooklyn. In 2011 they founded a design studio and have shown work with Moss, Phillips de Pury, The Future Perfect, Matter, all in New York; both Elemental, and Inventory Objects in Miami; Colectivo Amor de Madre, São Paulo; Museo di Arte Moderna e Contemporanea di Trento e Rovereto; and the Wunderkammer pavilion at the 2012 Venice Biennale.

chen-williams.com

Maartje Dros and François Lombarts

Dros's work is focused on the use and dynamics at the periphery of space and borders in the public realm. Her work creates collaboration between the user and the space rather than giving center stage simply to the object; it questions not only the hardware of our environment but the finished design can also be seen as an expression of social structures.

François Lombarts has been active as an independent designer since 2007. He focuses on physically experiencing, researching, and defining the various aspects of public space. His fascination with public space is especially rooted in its informal use, where everyday basic needs often manifest themselves in unstructured and informal ways. His designs strive to create situations and develop means in which this spontaneity can manifest itself.

www.maartjedros.nl

Sara Ebert

Ebert spent several years co-managing the family gallery before attending Pratt Institute to study industrial design. She currently calls Brooklyn, NY, home. Ebert's approach to design often involves merging her craft background with industrial methods and materials. She is inspired by forms and solutions found in nature, as well as the simplicity and efficiency of utilitarian objects. Above all, she reminds herself to never take her work too seriously, and strives to inject a dose of fun and beauty into all she does.

saraebert.com

Travis Ekmark

Travis works with design agencies, start-ups, nonprofits, and small businesses to create visual strategies, brand identities, user interfaces, and weird objects. His previous experience includes projects with Coca-Cola, College Board, Intel, and Scoutmob. He currently runs an anti-design office called Brothers with his business partner, Alvin Diec. He makes dystopian housewares under the name Object Trust with his business partner Collin Farill. He is also a co-founder of the Southern Design Concern and a member of the American Design Club. Educated at Georgia Tech, his approach to design is rooted in research, collaboration, and appropriation.

travisekmark.com

45 Kilo

The design studio 45 Kilo was founded in Berlin in 2007. Their work is focused on furniture and interior design and often combines industrialized production processes and materials with crafts, using a very simple, reduced visual language. The studio creates basic designs that reflect a functionalist and sometimes playful approach to everyday objects. They work both as a design studio, and as producers of custom-made furniture alongside a series of their own products.

www.45kilo.com

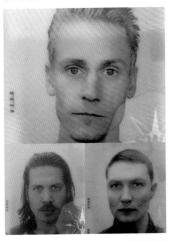

Daniel Franzén, Adam Almquist, Oscar Titelman

Born in 1972, Daniel Franzén is an interior architect. He studied at Konstfack University in Sweden, and Tohoku University of Art and Design in Japan. He set up the company TAF Architects with two friends in 2002 and ran this until 2005, after which he set up his own office—Bunker Hill—in order to focus on the projects that he finds most interesting and meaningful. He has designed jewelry worn by Swedish and international pop stars, the smallest apartment in Stockholm (at 11 square meters/118 square feet), modern barn houses, stores, and restaurants. He is also one of the most progressive users of Swedish pine, evidenced in such projects as the Blomkvist apartment in Stockholm, decorated almost entirely in pine plywood with a splash of marble. Franzén has exhibited in London, Paris, Tokyo, Berlin, and Milan.

Adam Almquist (born 1975) works as a designer and design strategist. He has previously worked as an antiques dealer and in fashion. He lives in Stockholm with his family, several dogs, and a horse.

Oscar Titelman (born 1975) is a former chef. He studied art and art history and has a bachelor's degree in industrial design. He is based in Stockholm, where he works as a product designer.

www.bunkerhill.se

Christian Halleröd

Christian Halleröd Design was founded in Stockholm, Sweden, in 1998. CHD works on a wide range of projects of varying scales, including product and furniture design, store concepts, and interior design. Their design strategy is rooted in a sensitivity to material choices. They also have extensive experience in the production and manufacturing process and always involve their clients, from the design conception stage through to product execution.

www.chd.se

Dominik Hehl

Dominik Hehl studied product design at the University of Applied Sciences in Potsdam and ECAL in Lausanne. After graduation in 2007 he designed a series of furniture pieces for family spaces and childcare. In 2008 Dominik assisted An Te Liu in the creation of "The Cloud" installation for the Venice Biennale. Before setting up his own studio in 2010, Dominik joined the Jerszy Seymour Design Workshop, and worked on product development for Magis (Flux Chair), Vitra, and Moulinex.

His studio projects range from customized furniture installations to serially manufactured products. One of his main interests is in designing and developing products and spaces for learning environments. His latest works are characterized by a very careful use of resources. The manufacturing processes of the Rohlingtisch result in very little waste, and the pieces all demonstrate how a seemingly rational approach can lead to playful designs with a joyful simplicity.

The Rohlingtisch is designed to be copied. So feel free to build, change, and enhance.

dominikhehl.de

Stephanie Hornig, Tine Huhn, Bodo Pahlke, Pascal Hien

Stephanie Hornig, Tine Huhn, Bodo Pahlke, and Pascal Hien formed a team for a one-week workshop during their studies at the Berlin University of the Arts. The project was awarded the first prize and resulted in a pop-up bookstore. Each of the four has now gone their own way. Tine Huhn and Stephanie Hornig finished their Diploma in Industrial Design in 2012. After working for Industrial Facility in London and Outofstock in Singapore, Tine Huhn is currently doing freelance work in Berlin. Stephanie Hornig is now based in London and works as a Junior Designer for Barber Osgerby. Bodo Pahlke worked for OFD studio in Stockholm before returning to Berlin to finish his studies as an industrial designer. After studying at ENSCI in Paris and working for the Arik Levy studio, Pascal Hien also returned to Berlin to finish his diploma at the University of the Arts.

www.stephaniehornig.com

Thomas Jenkins

Thomas Jenkins, born 1980, is a British designer based in Oslo, Norway. Thomas currently divides his time between his own studio and branding agency work. Thomas attended London South Bank University, and graduated with a first-class honors degree in Engineering Product Design in 2002. His career started immediately afterward, working for Dyson appliances, until 2006 when he moved to Oslo as a Senior Designer for Frost Produkt. In September 2008 he was invited to attend a summer school in the UK run by the Royal Designers for Industry. Here he worked with and learned from some of the UK's best designers and, following this, he was invited to become a fellow of the Royal Society of Arts. On his return to Oslo, Thomas began working on some self-initiated projects while freelancing for TBWA\Oslo. This continued until late 2011 when he was asked to run the MA design program at the National Academy for the Arts in Oslo (KHiO) for four months.

In his work, Thomas strives to create value by combining traditional craft with the best of today's manufacturing techniques and materials. He aims to create idealistic yet pragmatic solutions through playful yet functional objects.

thomasjenkins.co

Brendan Keim

Brendan is a Brooklyn-based artist and designer, raised on the shoreline of Connecticut. He attended Pratt Institute and completed a Bachelor's Degree in Industrial Design. After graduating in 2005, Brendan spent the next five years working with various designers and firms throughout the five boroughs, including Lindsey Adelman, Patrick Townsend, Clodagh, PICO, Keith Recker, and Nick Dine.

In 2012, Brendan received his Master's of Fine Arts at Rhode Island School of Design's Furniture program in Providence, RI.

www.brendankeim.com

Ladies & Gentlemen Studio

Founded by Dylan Davis and Jean Lee in 2010, Ladies & Gentlemen Studio's playful explorations in materiality blend their resourceful curiosity with the desire to find ideal pairings of material and function. The studio's open, multidisciplinary approach is fed by inspiration collected from their everyday discoveries, explorations, and surroundings. From these observations, L&G creates a diverse set of products, from small objects, to jewelry, furniture, lighting, and beyond.

Jean and Dylan met in 2002 while studying industrial design at the University of Washington. Their studies also took them to Rome and on travels throughout Italy and France. When they are not fixated on L&G design tasks, the pair spend time contributing to JOIN Design Seattle and Brite Collective, organizations with the mission to promote and advance independent design in the US Northwest. They also enjoy working on their home, gardening, traveling, and cooking.

ladiesandgentlemenstudio.com

Jonathan Legge

Jonathan Legge is a Creative Consultant working in London and Dublin. He is Founder and Creative Director of the Irish e-commerce company, Makers&Brothers. Before founding Makers&Brothers in 2011 he worked as a project designer with Ilse Crawford at Studioilse. During his five years there he led projects in London, Cambridge, Stockholm, and Newfoundland. During 2012 he was a guest tutor at the Royal College of Art. In recent years he has exhibited his work in New York, London, Milan, and Berlin. Jonathan studied at the Dublin Institute of Technology and then moved to London where he did a Master's in Design Products at the Royal College of Art, studying under Ron Arad.

www.makersandbrothers.com

Love Aesthetics

Love Aesthetics is a blog run by 24-year-old Ivania Carpio, who is based in the Netherlands. She has been running her blog for five years and she makes furniture, jewelry, and clothes. Ivania lives by the motto of "Less is More," but one look at her computer confirms her as a digital hoarder.

love-aesthetics.blogspot.co.uk

Naoya Matsuo

Naoya Matsuo was born in Tokyo. He studied design and learned welding there, then studied woodworking in London. After working for a designer's studio, he founded the studio Grand Furniture and Factory. He now runs his own workshop in Tokyo as a designer-maker. He exhibited XX as one of three knock-down furniture pieces at the 2011 Stockholm Furniture Fair. Every time he exhibits in foreign countries, he designs knock-down pieces and carries them all by hand to save costs.

www.naomat.jp

StudioMK27

StudioMK27 was founded at the beginning of the '80s by Marcio Kogan and today works with 20 architects, besides collaborators in numerous countries around the world. The architects of the studio develop the projects from start to finish, and sign as the projects co-authors. The studio has won numerous international awards such as: Wallpaper* Design Awards, Record House, Interior Record, D&AD, LEAF Awards, Dedalo Minosse, Barbara Cappochin of the International Biennial of Padova, Spark Awards, and World Architecture Festival. In 2011, *Wallpaper** and *Época* named Marcio Kogan as one of their 100 most influential people, and he received the title of honorary member of the AIA (American Institute of Architects) and in 2012 represented Brazil in the Venice Biennale. In Brazil he has received 13 awards from the Instituto de Arquitetos do Brasil (Brazilian Institute of Architects).

StudioMK27's projects are valued for their formal simplicity, always working with special attention to details and finishings. Marcio Kogan and the architects of the team, great admirers of the Brazilian modernist generation, seek to fulfill the difficult task of giving continuity to this line of production.

marciokogan.com.br

Blanca Ortiz

Born in Madrid in 1984, from an early age Blanca has been passionate about textures, colors, materials, and product design, especially furniture. After completing a degree in law she studied industrial design at the Istituto Europeo di Design and then began an internship with Ciszak Dalmas in Madrid, working on the creation of new furniture for the MAX&Co, Milan, and Madrid stores.

In 2012 she set up her own studio with two interior designers and they created an online platform called "Homeless Design Network: Objects Looking for a Home" that aims to promote responsible design and gives visibility to emerging designers, craftsmen, and small producers. They organize design exhibitions all around Europe, such as the "Homeless Design Competition" for the Salone del Mobile in Milan 2012, which had the Campana brothers as jurors. They also participated in the "Better World" exhibition at the 2012 Venice Biennale.

In addition, Blanca's personal work has been shown at several exhibitions, including "Decoracción" and "Hand in Hand" at Mad Gallery, both in Madrid.

www.intresign.com

Sarah Pease

Sarah is an independent designer, maker, and researcher. Through her work in all media, Sarah strives to create products that challenge notions of value and function. Her appreciation for straightforward thinking and efficient construction manifests itself in minimal aesthetics and intuitive interfaces. Sarah is a recent graduate of the Rhode Island School of Design, where she studied furniture and product design, with a heavy emphasis on craftsmanship and user interaction. She believes strongly in local manufacturing, and relies on the skilled craftspeople of New England to aid in the production of her work.

Sarah was recently noted in *Dwell* magazine as one of the "youngest and most promising designing minds at work today," and has been highlighted by *Core77* and Lifehacker for her work as a visiting student at the MIT Media Lab.

sarahpease.com

Chris Rucker

Chris Rucker graduated with a degree in sculpture from the University of Connecticut in Storrs, where he also grew up. He's been working in design and build in New York City for over 16 years, both under the name Ruckercorp and with his own firm, Ar & Dee, located in Brooklyn. The firm is a design collaboration between Chris and Rob Herschenfeld, the culmination of a decade of joint work on projects of all scales across many disciplines.

Adapting to a changing New York City, which has pushed out smaller design–build firms, the two have worked toward their shared vision of an environment that fosters design, craftsmanship, and apprentice-style training. Recognizing the lack of skilled designers with a firm knowledge of manufacturing techniques, and a shrinking pool of high-level fabricators in traditional woodwork, cabinet-making, welding, and machining, they took it all under one roof to encourage cross-disciplinary dialogue and training focused on the progress of individual craftsmen.

aranddee.net

Dik Scheepers

Dik Scheepers was born in Amstelveen, the Netherlands, in 1978 and studied product design at the Academy of Fine Arts in Maastricht. After graduating, Dik started his own studio in the south of the Netherlands where he now works on designing and making new products both in-house and on commission.

He works by trying, discarding, and experimenting with different materials and/or combinations, taking a design apart and putting it back together again differently. That, he believes, is how things evolve and new designs arise. The way a design has been made is as important to him as the end result—to think of a different way, simplifying matters in search of new possibilities.

dikscheepers.nl

Klemens Schillinger

Klemens Schillinger is an independent designer from Austria who currently lives and works in London. After graduating from the Royal College of Art in 2011 he has been working as a freelance designer for various design studios as well as carrying on with his own work. In general his work engages with art, design, craft, co-creation, ad-hocism, and DIY. His products revolve around transparency in terms of manufacture, clarity of form, material, and content, but also humor. He aims to develop simple yet carefully thought-out products, design methods, and DIY recipes, which intend to capture and acknowledge imperfections and unpredictable outcomes.

www.klemensschillinger.com